Violence and Nonviolence

Studies in Social, Political, and Legal Philosophy
Series Editor: James P. Sterba, University of Notre Dame

This long-standing Rowman & Littlefield philosophy series critically analyzes and evaluates the major social, political, and legal ideals, institutions, and practices of our time. **James P. Sterba**, past president of the American Philosophical Association's Central Division, and widely known and respected public philosopher throughout the world, brings dynamic, leading voices to bear on important and provocative topics, demonstrating the value of philosophical thinking in responding to contemporary issues.

Titles in the Series

Heirs of Oppression: Racism and Reparations (2010) by J. Angelo Corlett
Ethics for Disaster (2009) by Naomi Zack
Moral Vision: How Everyday Life Shapes Ethical Thinking (2005) by Duane L. Cady
Linking Visions: Feminist Bioethics, Human Rights, and the Developing World (2004), edited by Rosemarie Tong, Anne Donchin, and Susan Dodds
Putting Humans First: Why We Are Nature's Favorite (2004) by Tibor R. Machan
Exploitation: What It Is and Why It's Wrong (2003) by Ruth J. Sample
American Heat: Ethical Problems with the United States' Response to Global Warming (2002) by Donald A. Brown
Just Ecological Integrity: The Ethics of Maintaining Planetary Life (2002), edited by Peter Miller and Laura Westra
Theorizing Backlash: Philosophical Reflections on the Resistance to Feminism (2002), edited by Anita M. Superson and Ann E. Cudd
Faces of Environmental Racism: Confronting Issues of Global Justice, 2nd edition (2001), edited by Laura Westra and Bill Lawson
Controversies in Feminism (2000), edited by James P. Sterba
Ecofeminist Philosophy: A Western Perspective on What It Is and Why It Matters (2000) by Karen J. Warren
The Idea of a Political Liberalism: Essays on Rawls (2000), edited by Victoria Davion and Clark Wolf
Self-Management and the Crisis of Socialism: The Rose in the Fist of the Present (2000) by Michael W. Howard
Gewirth: Critical Essays on Action, Rationality, and Community (1999), edited by Michael Boylan
Same Sex: Debating the Ethics, Science, and Culture of Homosexuality (1997), edited by John Corvino

Violence and Nonviolence

An Introduction

Barry L. Gan

ROWMAN & LITTLEFIELD
Lanham • Boulder • New York • Toronto • Plymouth, UK

Published by Rowman & Littlefield
4501 Forbes Boulevard, Suite 200, Lanham, Maryland 20706
www.rowman.com

10 Thornbury Road, Plymouth PL6 7PP, United Kingdom

British Library Cataloguing in Publication Information Available

Library of Congress Cataloging-in-Publication Data

Gan, Barry L., 1948-
Violence and nonviolence : an introduction / Barry L. Gan.
pages cm. -- (Studies in social, political, and legal philosophy)
Includes bibliographical references and index.
ISBN 978-1-4422-1759-1 (cloth : alk. paper) -- ISBN 978-1-4422-1760-7 (pbk. : alk. paper) -- ISBN 978-1-4422-1761-4 (electronic) 1. Violence. 2. Nonviolence. I. Title.
HM886.G36 2013
303.6--dc23
2013012113

∞™ The paper used in this publication meets the minimum requirements of American National Standard for Information Sciences Permanence of Paper for Printed Library Materials, ANSI/NISO Z39.48-1992.

Printed in the United States of America

For my children, Hilary and Reid

Contents

Acknowledgments

Many people have given me encouragement, support, and suggestions along the way in the development of this book. Numerous friends and several organizations figure prominently among those who have listened to and read various parts of this book since it was first conceived around 1998. Given that this book was fourteen years in its conception and development, I have probably forgotten to include names of some of those to whom I owe thanks, and I apologize for such omissions.

The Peace and Justice Studies Association (formerly COPRED and the Peace Studies Association) offered many venues throughout the years where I could meet with people, proffer ideas, and receive constructive criticism and suggestions. Tom Hastings and Michael Nagler have been particularly helpful to me as I developed my ideas throughout the years of my association with PJSA and its precursors. I am grateful to them for their advice, encouragement, and friendship.

Others who deserve thanks include Bart Gruzalski as well as Susan Anderson, a colleague at St. Bonaventure University who read quite carefully an early version of this manuscript and made meticulous notes and suggestions for me. Likewise, I want to thank the folks at the International Center on Nonviolent Conflict, Jack DuVall in particular, who with warmth and friendship opened up new doors for me and enabled me to explore, debate, and articulate the practical side of nonviolent action on a more global scale.

Concerned Philosophers for Peace (CPP) has offered annual conferences at which I was able to trot out, tentatively at first, the ideas that formed the basis for each of the chapters in this book. Chief among the friends and colleagues in CPP who offered advice along the way are Rob Gildert, Bill Gay, Laura Duhan Kaplan, Wendy Hamblet, Ron Glossop, Paul Churchill, Dennis Rothermel, Gail Presbey, Jan Narveson, Trudy Govier, Bill Gay, and Ron Hirschbein, who I understand may have been one of the reviewers of this book for Rowman & Littlefield.

I owe many thanks to Jim Sterba, a former president of CPP, who read my manuscript and said to me that the manuscript needed to be in print. He bent his efforts to bring my manuscript to the attention of a few editors, and the upshot of his efforts is that the manuscript is being published, thanks in great measure to the value he saw in it.

My good friends Andy Fitz-Gibbon, Predrag Cicovacki, and Rick Werner, also members of CPP, have provided me with many, many hours of conversations over the years about the ideas that this book comprises. Their conversations were always stimulating and reinforcing. But most especially among the members (and former presidents of CPP) I would like to thank two people who have not only been dear friends but teachers, informally in the case of one, Duane Cady, informally and formally in the case of the other, Bob Holmes.

Duane Cady and I sat on the front lawn of the Fellowship of Reconciliation in Nyack, New York, in the late 1990s, and he listened attentively to my sketch of an idea for this book. He was excited about the sketch and encouraged me to move ahead, offering me stories of some of his own trials and tribulations in the publishing realm. Years later, initially without my knowing it, he was an early reviewer of my manuscript, and his insights and suggestions helped very much with my later revisions to a penultimate manuscript.

Bob Holmes has been a dear friend and mentor for many years. He was one of my professors in both undergraduate and, years later, graduate school, and I have used many of his ideas in the development of my own, as anyone who reads this book will see. But he has also been a close friend and adviser over the past twenty years, and his edits of some of my chapters, my conversations with him about many of my ideas over the past thirty years, and his gentle encouragement during these decades have all been central to my own development as a thinker about nonviolence.

My wife and partner for thirty years until recently, Maureen Bernas, supported me for years in my efforts to complete a working manuscript, discussing many of my ideas with me and offering philosophical and editorial advice. In particular, I recall her saying to me at the outset of one of my sabbaticals, "Do you want to write a book for professional philosophers, or do you want to write a book for a wider audience?" Her question was a bit more pointed than that, but the discussions that followed caused me to write a very different book, the book that this has become, and I thank her for helping me find that direction and orientation. It was an invaluable insight, one that ultimately is responsible for this book being accepted for publication.

My son, Reid, has challenged me with his ideas and behavior over the years, from his early years of refusing to sit still in a stroller to his later years of engagement in a physically rough Division I soccer team. Frequently I was forced to balance my urge to control and direct him with my recognition of the value of his personal autonomy. The internal struggle that he often helped to precipitate in me has also been instrumental in the formation of ideas present in this book. Always, I can say happily, he emerged as a person more than worthy of the trust that I, and others, placed in him.

Finally, my daughter, Hilary, read an early version of this book and provided me with many critical insights. She urged me to speak in a more direct voice and gave me the idea of beginning some chapters with a poignant anecdote or epigraph. I am thankful to her for her suggestions, perceptions, encouragement, and enthusiasm. She coined the sentence that for me distinguishes comprehensive from selective nonviolence and serves as the subheading for the very last short section in the book: "If it's about winning, it's not nonviolence."

I

Violence

Chapter One

Molded by Myths

My wife once lost her wallet. She and I searched everywhere for it—under the car seats, under the couches, under the bed, in the laundry basket, at work. For days neither of us was able to find it, but she was sure that it hadn't been stolen, was sure that she had either lost or misplaced it. Finally we thought very methodically about where she had been the day before she discovered it missing, and we recalled that on that day she had been locked out of our house and had managed to break in by crawling through a basement window. We walked down to the basement and looked beneath that window, and there, on the ground in a corner of a damp cellar where we otherwise would never have thought to look for a wallet, we found it.

The point here is that when we look for something we have lost, we first decide where we might have misplaced it, and then we begin to search. However, if we are wrong in our assumptions about where we lost it, we fail to find it. Our likelihood of success is determined by our initial assumptions. This observation illustrates the central and noncontroversial point of the first part of this book: that our assumptions govern or direct our individual behaviors, and the assumptions of a community or a society govern or direct its social, political, and economic behaviors and policies.

Just as our initial assumptions about where the wallet might have been lost prevented us at first from finding it, so the beliefs that people unquestioningly accept often prevent them from addressing successfully their own problems. Like our initial assumptions about where my wife lost her wallet, some personal and societal beliefs and assumptions are misleading. And because they are misleading, because they may be false or mistaken, these assumptions are often themselves the source of many personal and social problems. To the extent that these misleading, false, or mistaken beliefs and assumptions are embedded in a personality or society, they can become so powerful that they underpin and undermine the very character of a personality or society, explaining and justifying unhelpful behaviors and policies. When entire cultures address their problems by relying on such assumptions, by relying on fictions as facts and by appealing to these fictions to justify actions, shaping their entire approach to problem solving, these beliefs and assumptions are best regarded as myths.

How do such myths operate at a societal or cultural level? One example of such a myth operating at a cultural level, in contrast to the mistaken assumptions that initially guided my wife's and my individual behaviors in the search for her wallet, was the widespread but mistaken belief in the middle of the fourteenth century that Jews were responsible for the Black Death, bubonic plague. Many Jews did not drink out of public wells because of Jewish dietary laws, and when people who used the public wells began dying of the plague, rumors spread that Jews had poisoned the wells. Jews were tortured to extract confessions, and under torture some Jews confessed to poisoning the wells. Word of the confessions spread, and Jews were banned from cities or killed outright. In Basel, Switzerland, in 1349, Christian townsfolk assembled an entire community of Jews and burned them to death. Throughout Germany, France, and Switzerland entire villages of Jews were attacked; in many places the property of Jews was confiscated; Jews were urged to convert to Christianity. It didn't matter that many Jews also died of the plague. This myth and the actions undertaken in its name served to reassure and validate, to justify and explain, the fears, behaviors, and policies of frightened populations. It didn't matter that the Pope himself spoke against the murder of the Jews. European society had a problem, a myth existed regarding the source of that problem, and people acted on the basis of that myth in ways that could be expected or predicted, given their belief in the myth. [1]

Belief in this myth caused other sorts of harm, too. It interfered with discovery of the truth. Easier to blame the plague on what was convenient to believe, on the intentional actions or malice of others who were different, on people to whom one was financially indebted. Why overturn assumptions and look at the problem from an entirely new perspective? It was easier to blame others for poisoning wells than to look at one's own conduct, one's own negligence, or one's own garbage and find the real culprit, the bacillus transmitted by fleas from rodents to people. It was easier to rely on existing myths to explain and justify one's behavior than it was to search for new answers. And if the solutions did not work at first, then, the myth suggested, the solutions simply needed to be pursued more vigorously.

An important aspect of such myths as these is the great conviction with which sincere and concerned people hold them. While many people may have exploited hatred and fear of Jews for personal gain or out of sheer malice, still more people, people of good will and noble intentions, fell prey to the power of such a myth. *Acting upon the false assumptions that these myths entailed, well-intentioned people did much harm.*

The United States, indeed the entire world, is itself under the spell of several extraordinarily powerful myths about violence. These myths—fictions or, at best, half-truths—permeate the thinking of the noblest people among us, influencing the decisions of the best-intentioned parents, politicians, philosophers, and officials throughout the legal system. These myths shape individuals and cultures, provide a distorted view of reality, justify and explain actions, and ultimately prevent people from addressing effectively the disease that we call violence. Ultimately they keep us from discovering the truth about violence; they keep us from successfully reducing violence. We seek to blame others for the violence in our culture rather than look to ourselves as responsible parties. We pursue failed policies more vigorously in the mistaken belief that we simply have not pursued present policies vigorously enough. And so we attempt to address the problem of violence in self-defeating ways, only within a narrow range of solutions. And good people thereby do much harm.

Evidence regarding the rates of violent crime is inconclusive. Violent crime in general decreased precipitously in Europe and the United States beginning around 1830. Violent crimes tended to decrease during periods of wartime (when those of an age most prone to violence are serving in the armed forces elsewhere) and tended to increase following wartime, presumably, it has been argued, because of war's legitimization of violence. Violence reached a new peak in the United States in the 1960s, after which it soared for thirty years. In the past fifteen to twenty years, however, the violent crime rate has dropped back to the levels of the 1960s, a substantial drop in the short term but less noticeable when looking at centuries-long trends.[2] In a similar way, until about 1970, prison incarceration rates in the United States hovered between 95 and 135 per 100,000 people. But beginning in 1972, incarceration rates began to rise until by 2007, they had reached 502 per 100,000 people, four to five times the rate of four decades earlier.[3] The number is now more than 700 per 100,000.[4]

Wars and war-related deaths are even more alarming. In the past one hundred years, on average, wars around the world have killed thirteen times as many people (over one million people annually) as, on average, wars have killed in the previous four hundred years (75,000 annually). Worse, most of the victims in earlier centuries were soldiers. But in the twentieth century that changed. During the first half of the twentieth century, one out of every two people killed as a result of war was a soldier. By the 1990s, for every eight people killed as a result of war, only one was a soldier. That is, nowadays, seven out of eight people killed as a result of war are not soldiers but, rather, they are noncombatants.[5]

Around the world people and nations regularly employ violence in the hope that the use of some violence will reduce or eliminate greater violence. For example, in an effort to protect its citizens from harm, the United States maintains the largest military force in the world, at a cost of approximately $700 billion per year, more than the military expenditures of all other nations combined. It has used its military forces more than one hundred times in the past one hundred years.[6] In an effort to make its streets safe, the United States imprisons more people than any other country in the world, more people, for example, than China, and not just *per capita*, but in actual numbers.[7] The United States has consistently ranked high among the nations that execute people, right up near the top with China, Iran, Pakistan, and Saudi Arabia.[8] Surprisingly, despite these efforts, the United States has a higher homicide rate than any European nation,[9] and its government was unable to prevent the attacks on September 11, 2001.

Part of the problem with these policies and behaviors is that people either resist acknowledging as violent the policies of their government or, when they do, they regard those policies as excusable or justifiable violence. This resistance amounts to a failure to recognize violence as violence. The willingness or readiness to excuse or justify violent behaviors sustains and is sustained by several other myths about the nature of violence, the nature of people, the use of violence, and the benefits of violence in general and punishment in particular. These myths limit our vision and help to perpetuate the violence in our society. In much the same way that people in the fourteenth century became convinced that Jews were responsible for the Black Death, we convince ourselves that these myths are true and are not plausibly open to question.

While few of us would deny the noncontroversial points of the first part of this book, that our assumptions govern or direct our individual behaviors, and that the assumptions of a community or a society govern or direct its social, political, and economic behaviors and policies, most of us are unwilling to accept that our beliefs about violence in particular are mistaken, that they are myths that perpetuate so many problems that we face. But that is precisely the second and more controversial point of the first part of this book.

Like the myths about the Black Death, the myths that underpin our culture are indeed unfounded assumptions, mistaken beliefs; and our commitment to them is a good part of the reason why our society is so violent. For this reason they are best regarded as violent myths. What, specifically, are these myths?

1. First, we believe that violence is primarily and most often physical. Typically we understand violence as comprising physical acts against other people's bodies or possessions: assault, robbery, murder, and rape, for example.
2. Second, we believe that some people are inherently evil, or—a variant of this myth—that people are innately aggressive or violent or evil and that there is nothing we can do about that fact. Typically we categorize people into two classes: those who are essentially good and those who are essentially bad.
3. Third, we believe that violence is sometimes necessary to prevent violence. Again, typically we justify violence to prevent violence because we believe that it is unfair that we who are good, we who are innocent, should have to suffer needlessly to stop violence or harm from befalling us. We also believe that a little bit of well-intentioned violence goes a long way toward preventing more extensive and malicious violence.
4. Fourth, we believe that one should not have to suffer for the wrongs of others, that it is wrongdoers who must suffer, wrongdoers who must be punished in order to set the world aright. The idea that people can be redeemed by making *them* suffer for their wrongdoing is widely accepted despite its flying in the face of

much empirical evidence as well as many religious teachings, most notably the redemptive suffering of Jesus.

5. Fifth, we believe that the use of nonviolence is either the coward's way out or, if not that, then we believe that nonviolence is ineffective in addressing violence and injustice.

The few people who challenge these myths are usually looked at as odd, idealistic, or mildly deranged. But people who are able to dismiss these violent myths and live their lives according to a different point of view are for the most part able to live nonviolently, even in a violent society. They approach problems, especially problems of violence, quite differently from the rest of us. Their lives and the lives of those around them are better for it, for they approach life from an alternative paradigm, a point of view borrowed from people like Jesus, Gandhi, Martin Luther King, Jr., and others, whose vision of a just and peaceful world rested on a different set of assumptions, a set of assumptions essentially nonviolent. The lives and accomplishments of these people exemplify another controversial point that the second part of this book puts forward, namely, that it is possible to function effectively and nonviolently in stark opposition to these myths that we so easily accept.

Here, however, a caution is necessary: it is tempting, when confronting these myths, to assert that their opposites are absolutely and always true, to say, for instance, that violence is never necessary to prevent violence or to say that one should never punish a wrongdoer. Such extreme or absolute claims are probably false as well, but one shouldn't conclude that because the extreme or absolute claims are false, so are milder, less extreme claims that point in a new and different direction.[10] This can't be too strongly emphasized: *to focus on the occasional exceptions, to focus on the few instances where violence might be necessary or where punishment might serve a useful purpose, is to ignore the overwhelming evidence that by and large, violence does not prevent violence, punishment does not serve a useful purpose, and so on. It is to ignore the overwhelming evidence that the myths outlined above are false, that they do not serve individuals, communities, or the world well at all.*

In the pages that follow, we shall see just what is wrong with each of these myths, and then we shall examine and develop alternative approaches to addressing the scourge of violence, approaches that are but a beginning, to be sure, but a beginning that is a seed from which we can harvest a nonviolent life, a nonviolent community, and a nonviolent world.

NOTES

1. See Barbara W. Tuchman, *A Distant Mirror* (New York: Alfred A. Knopf, 1978), 117–21; and also Paul Johnson, *A History of the Jews* (New York: Harper Perennial, 1987), 216–17.

2. See Ted Robert Gurr, "Historical Trends in Violent Crime: A Critical Review of the Evidence," *Crime and Justice* 3 (1981), 295–353; and also "Key Facts at a Glance: Violent Crime Trends, National Crime Victimization Survey Violent Crime Trends, 1973–2008," Bureau of Justice Statistics,http://bjs.ojp.usdoj.gov/content/glance/tables/viortrdtab.cfm (accessed May 20, 2012).

3. Franklin E. Zimring, "The Scale of Imprisonment in the United States: Twentieth Century Patterns and Twenty-First Century Prospects," *The Journal of Criminal Law and Criminology* 100, no. 3 (2010): 1227–31.

4. Adam Liptak, "U.S. Prison Population Dwarfs That of Other Nations," *The New York Times*, April 23, 2008, http://www.nytimes.com/2008/04/23/world/americas/23iht23prison.12253738.html?pagewanted=all (accessed May 15, 2012).

5. Ruth Leger Sivard, *World Military and Social Expenditures 1991* (Washington, D.C. : World Priorities, 1991), 20.

6. Zoltan Grossman, "From Wounded Knee to Iraq: A Century of American Military Intervention," http://academic.evergreen.edu/g/grossmaz/interventions.html (accessed on May 26, 2009).

7. Liptak, "U.S. Prison Population."

8. Amnesty International, "The Death Penalty in 2008," http://www.amnesty.org/en/death-penalty/death-sentences-and-executions-in-2008 (accessed on May 26, 2009).

9. *Global Burden of Armed Violence 2008*, Geneva Declaration on Armed Violence and Development, http://www.genevadeclaration.org/fileadmin/docs/Global-Burden-of-Armed-Violence-full-report.pdf (accessed May 26, 2009), 71.

10. See, for example, Andrew Fiala, "Pacifism and the Trolley Problem," *The Acorn: Journal of the Gandhi King Society* 15, no. 1 (2013).

Chapter Two

The Myth of Physical Violence

In 1968 a woman in her early twenties and living with her parents in Tempe, Arizona, came home one morning and admitted that she had spent the night with a married man, an Air Force officer. Angered and determined to teach the young woman a lesson, her parents loaded their daughter and her pet dog in a car and drove out to the desert, where they handed the girl a shovel and told her to dig a shallow grave for her dog. When she had dug the hole, the parents handed the girl a gun. Then the mother held the dog, and the parents ordered her to shoot the dog and bury it as her punishment. At this point the young woman put the gun to her head and shot herself to death. [1]

This account highlights the central theme of this chapter: that it is crucial for us to recognize that one can do serious harm to others without ever assaulting them physically. This fact has two important implications. First, violence does not consist of the physical injury done to others but is in the mind of the perpetrator, in the perpetrator's intent to harm or to act in a way that is reasonably foreseeable to cause harm, physical or otherwise. Second, our failure to appreciate this central aspect of violence prevents us from recognizing most violence as violence, let alone addressing it responsibly, effectively, and adequately.

Chapter 2

THE COMMON VIEW

Typically when we think about violence, among the first images to come to mind are those of violent crime: murders, muggings, rapes, child abuse, wife beatings, the stuff with which television, movies, and news inundate us. Often, too, when we think of violence, we think of war—land mines maiming innocents, mortar shells falling in Kosovo or roadside bombs exploding in Afghanistan, smart bombs, depleted uranium munitions, machete-wielding murderers in Rwanda or Algeria, drones targeting unsuspecting conspirators, or guerrillas and paramilitary forces overrunning villages or hauling people out of bed late at night to assassinate them.

These images reflect media content and lend much support to the idea that violence is the infliction of physical harm. Recent events add further force to this idea. Since the September 11, 2001, attacks on the World Trade Center and the Pentagon, governments and news media have focused more on the violence they call terrorism. The term *violence* now calls to mind horrid pictures of airliners crashing into towers, germ-laden letters being sent through the mail, explosives-filled vehicles crashing through barricades, or mass murders of schoolchildren.

THE PROBLEM WITH THE COMMON VIEW

These typical examples of violence are obvious because they are the most extreme forms of violence. However, they are not the most common forms of violence. One's eye is naturally drawn to the brightest object in a painting or the brightest light in a room, even though there may be many other objects in the painting or many other lights in a room. Similarly with violence: violence maims or kills many people, and the most vivid forms of violence distract our attention from the more frequent, far subtler, less visible forms.

By focusing on the more obvious examples of violence, violence in which most people do not engage most of the time, we allow ourselves to think that we are not violent when in fact we are, far more often than we are willing to acknowledge. This allows us to see the problem of violence as the fault of others, not ourselves. And in this way the problem is largely ignored.

Terrorism illustrates this point well. Although thousands died in the September, 11, 2001, attacks on the World Trade Center and the Pentagon, the terrorism lay not so much in the death and destruction of September 11 but in the fear that such attacks instilled in the rest of the world and the United States in particular and especially. That fear, not the initial physical harm but the mental or psychological stress that the attacks imposed on survivors, is the heart of terrorism. More people have been harmed by the psychological stress caused by these attacks than were physically harmed by the terrorist attacks themselves. This is not to say that the psychological harm affects people more severely than the physical harm; sometimes it does, sometimes it does not. But the psychological trauma tends to be minimized or overlooked when placed alongside the physical harm, even though the psychological harm affects more people more often.

Other examples are similarly instructive. When, for example, Palestinian suicide bombers blow themselves up and kill others around them, the physical harm is immediate and intense. But the psychological trauma that affects family members of those who were killed, the fear that infects the rest of the society, though not as immediate or intense, is real enough. And it affects far more people. Similarly, when Israeli bulldozers clear one Palestinian home, the effect is severe on the home's inhabitants, but the trauma that such an action causes on other homeowners, however subtle, is far more widespread. People alter their behaviors because of the psychological effect that harm to others has upon them.

The situation is very much the same for violence perpetrated upon an individual. Although a husband who abuses his wife by physically assaulting her may do so only every few weeks or months, the violence is not solely or even primarily in the beating: it is in the production of constant anxiety with which the wife tiptoes around the home in the periods between the beatings, when the husband's glance is a threat, his attitude a condemnation. The doing of violence is in the sense of worthlessness that he conveys to his wife, not merely at the moments when he strikes her but at all the times in between. The wife's behavior patterns are altered dramatically from what they would be under normal conditions.

When one person lies to another or deceives another, harm is perpetrated in at least two ways. The person to whom the lie is told chooses to act on the basis of the information in that lie, and that person thereby functions with misinformation, functions in a way he or she may very well have chosen not to function had the truth been known. The person who tells the lie becomes, in essence, two people: the person who knows he lied and the person he must appear to be in order to maintain the lie. He has divided his personality.

Violence can be subtler still. Some years back, when I was about to take my son to school one day, he told me that his eyes were itching. He needed some allergy medicine. We returned home and I searched high and low for the medicine. I began swearing: I was angry with my wife, thinking she had not returned the bottle to where it belonged. I was frustrated over not being able to find it because my son might be late for school and I might be late for the class I had to teach in twenty minutes. I was aware that I was making my son nervous by my swearing and stomping about the house. I was angry with myself for making my son nervous. I was getting angrier and angrier by the minute. I called my wife at her place of work. "Where's the medicine?!" I demanded. "Did you try the medicine cabinet?" she suggested. "Yes! I tried the medicine cabinet," I huffed back. "How about the kitchen cupboard?" she offered. "Yes!" I replied with increasing exasperation. Well, I never found it. I charged back out to the car and begin backing out of the driveway. . . . Down the street comes the little beige car driven ever so slowly each morning by the old man who lived three doors down the street from us. It was just about time for school to begin, and I could not back out of my driveway fast enough to beat this beige car puttering down the street. He is ahead of me now, and I am riding the gas pedal and the brake, tailgating him. I'm cursing him aloud. My son looks over at me and quietly says, "Dad, my eyes aren't itching anymore."

They were itching, still, most likely, but he didn't care or no longer noticed. To him, and to myself, I was the bigger problem. I was behaving violently even though I wasn't physically assaulting anyone. I was doling out violence to any number of people. Did I think my wife didn't sense my anger, think that she didn't tense up when she heard me like that? And my son? Or the driver in front of me on the road? I didn't make this story up. It happened, and the only thing that stopped me in my tracks was a friend of mine on the sidewalk. He was walking his son to school, and he saw me swearing at the driver in front of me. He ascertained the situation immediately, pointed to me, and began laughing at me. I stopped, embarrassed and ashamed of myself.

BUT WHERE IS THE VIOLENCE IN THESE EXAMPLES?

Some people object to the use of the term *violence* to describe these later examples. They might call such behaviors abusive or threatening but would resist labeling them as violent. They would say that violence is simply the physical act of injuring or threatening to injure another person. They would say that actions that do not involve the use or threatened use of physical force are not violent actions.[2]

This is the common understanding of violence, but as I've been arguing, it is flawed. On the one hand, it excludes certain acts that anyone would consider acts of violence. On the other hand, it includes certain actions that few would regard as violent acts.

Consider a series of famous experiments conducted in the early 1960s by Stanley Milgram, experiments that were duplicated with variations in the years that followed before this kind of experiment came to be regarded as unethical.[3] In the first of these experiments Milgram invited volunteers to participate in a psychology experiment. The volunteers were told that it was an experiment on how people learn, but in reality it was an experiment on how easily people obey orders. He asked volunteers to draw slips of paper that would identify them either as a teacher or a student. The volunteers did not know, however, that half of the people in their group were in fact not volunteers. They were people pretending to be volunteers, and they all claimed to draw slips as students. The actual volunteers all drew slips as teachers. The actual volunteers were told that they would be testing how fast the other "volunteers," the fake volunteers, could learn. They were told that they would be helping them to learn by giving them small electric shocks whenever they answered a question wrong. The students were wired, but unknown to the volunteers, the "teachers," the wires were not actually connected to any electricity. Nonetheless, each time a "teacher" saw a question answered incorrectly, he or she was instructed to give a jolt of electricity to the "student" he or she was monitoring. The "teachers" could see on a dial the level of shock they were administering, from very mild to lethal. As the numbers of wrong answers increased, the "teachers" were encouraged to give more severe shocks. When the "teachers" hesitated to do so, the experimenters encouraged them and reassured them that it was all right, despite the screams that they would hear coming from the "students." Milgram and others repeated this experiment in various forms, always with the same results: most of the subjects in the experiment, the "teachers," were relatively easily encouraged to administer what they believed to be lethal shocks to the students.[4]

Milgram conducted these experiments (now considered unethical) in an effort to understand how it was that so many German soldiers could have been willing to take the lives of so many innocent civilians in concentration camps. He got his answer. But his answer is instructive for our purposes, too. Were the "teachers" engaging in violent actions? Were they acting violently even though the subjects, it turns out, were not harmed? The answer to this question is problematic. On the one hand, we are inclined to say that they were acting violently because they administered what they believed were lethal electric shocks to people who were not themselves causing anyone any harm. On the other hand, we want to say that there was no violence because nobody was harmed. What is the truth of the matter? Before answering this question, consider another example.

Suppose you are involved in an auto accident that is the result of something completely beyond your control. Suppose that while driving one night, sober and alert, you drive over a patch of ice on a bridge and skid sideways across an oncoming lane of traffic, striking another car and killing the driver. Although the other driver was certainly harmed, although we might say that the other driver died a violent death, few of us would accuse you of performing a violent act.

Robert Holmes captures this point well. After making a number of distinctions about the ways in which the term *violence* is used, he says: "Language has a convenient resource for enabling us to distinguish these different modes of violence. It is in the idea of 'doing violence.'"[5] A dentist who accidentally fractures a patient's jaw performs an act that is violent, but the dentist has not *done* violence to her patient unless she intended to harm the patient or acted recklessly. The accidental discharge of my gun that results in injury to my friend is indeed a violent event, but I didn't *do* violence to my friend unless I intended to harm him or acted recklessly.

The point is this: in trying to understand violence as a human phenomenon, there is nothing to be gained by studying genuine *accidents*; the point is to understand how and why human beings *perpetrate* violence. Yes, we call tornadoes violent, and we call car accidents violent, but there is a difference between a violent event and a violent action, and the difference lies in human intention and motivation. *Doing* violence has more to do with intent and less to do with outcome. The story of a person who accidentally precipitates a violent outcome is not the story of a person who has performed a violent act. But the story of a person who knowingly acts in a way that is likely to precipitate harm, whether or not that person is successful, is the story of a person doing violence. Successfully addressing the scourge of violence demands that we acknowledge this difference and focus on the doing of violence and not on events that happen to have a merely violent aspect to them.

However, many understand the doing of violence as the "application of physical force with intent to harm, and typically, the physical effect of damage, destruction, injury or killing."[6] Such an understanding is insufficient. As Holmes says,

> Consider the debilitating effects of prolonged and intensive brainwashing, or of ghetto schools upon young children, or of the continual humiliation and debasement of a child by parents. In none of these cases need physical violence be used. But in each case violence is done, and of a sort that may be far more injurious than most physical violence.[7]

Or consider the example offered at the outset of this chapter, that of the girl whose parents had her dig a grave for her dog and who shot herself rather than kill her dog. Writing of this episode, Newton Garver points out that the parents had not inflicted any physical injury on their daughter; she had done that all by herself. Nor had they in any way forced her to shoot herself. She was in some sense free not to do so. But clearly, he says, they had done violence to her in some basic way. They had violated her status as a person.[8]

A CONFUSION?

But perhaps this view of violence confuses the cause of violence with the violence itself. Perhaps the violence is the physical force or effect itself, and the intent that precedes it might more properly be regarded as the cause or source of the violence. Perhaps it is useful to address violence by focusing on its causes or sources but recognize that these are not the violence itself. Perhaps, too, this so-called psychological violence is simply a prelude to violence, a causal factor that sometimes contributes to violence and sometimes does not. Some might say that my anger over not being able to find my son's medicine, for example, might best be called anger or annoyance or frustration, but not psychological violence.[9] Though one's anger or frustration might precipitate physical violence toward others, it might nonetheless be misleading to call that anger or frustration by the term *violence*.

These concerns are understandable, but they miss the points just made. Whether or not one commits an act of violence actually has nothing to do with the type of act performed. The doing of violence is not the mere performance of some action: if I accidentally but not recklessly discharge a gun, I do not thereby commit an act of violence. But if I deliberately discharge it with intent to harm, or if I vent my anger in ways that I know make those around me unsettled at best, I am doing violence. A person who intends to assassinate a political leader might fire a rifle with a silencer at the leader and miss hitting the leader. Perhaps no one ever becomes aware of the act. Shall we say that the inept assassin did not perform an act of violence? Quite the contrary. He performed a violent act. It caused no harm to the intended victim, but it was a violent act. Doing violence is the carrying out of an intention in an action likely to cause harm. Any actual harm that results from that is a by-product and not the true locus of violence. How the intention is carried out is irrelevant. Whether or not it succeeds is irrelevant.

The term *violence* is, in fact, rooted in the concept of violation. Michael N. Nagler, in his book *Is There No Other Way?*, says that the Latin term *violare* originally meant "to bear in on with force" and later meant "to injure, dishonor, outrage, violate." [10] He says: "The lion does not 'dishonor, outrage, or violate' the lamb that instinct drives it to kill. . . . There is no bond between the lion and the lamb that is torn asunder when the predator strikes. . . . Violence as we mean the term is a human phenomenon. . . . Violence tears the fabric of life." [11]

Notice that while it might be correct to say that the lamb died a violent death, it would stretch somewhat the notion of *doing violence* to say the lion did violence to the lamb. The notion of *doing violence* involves carrying out an intention and then acting on that intention with some sort of awareness that acting on that intention is likely to make another worse off against their wishes. The lion, presumably, is not capable of framing such an intention. Only if it has such a capability can it do violence.

Nagler also points out that the Sanskrit word for violence, *himsa*, strictly speaking, does not mean the act of striking or slaying: "It means the *desire* or intention to do the act, in this case injure" (italics his). [12] This etymology suggests, then, that violence is not the act that arises from one's intentions; it is, according to Sanskrit etymology, the intention itself which, when manifested in action, amounts to doing violence. Thus, the concept of violence in human action is much more closely tied to the intention to do harm than it is tied to the particular means by which that intention manifests itself.

Why care about such details? It is important to be clear about the difference between *violence* and *doing violence*. If we remain careless with our use of the terms, we will continue to focus only on the most obvious instances of doing violence, missing the more common instances, including especially our own. And then we will not address adequately the problem of violence.

CONCLUSION

What, then, can we conclude about the nature of violence?

The only element common to all of the scenarios that most people would call *doing violence* is the intention to act in a way likely to cause harm. The differences are in the means employed and the outcomes obtained. The means and outcomes are incidental, quite literally, for all intents and purposes. Yet it is precisely on the means and the outcomes that studies of violence have largely focused, thereby ignoring the heart and soul of violence! If we focus on incidentals, we miss the crux. *To do violence is to carry out an intention to behave in a manner likely to cause harm.* This account is ambiguous, but deliberately so. One can intend to cause harm, in which case when one acts according to that intention, one behaves, intentionally, with the aim of causing harm. Nagler argues similarly: "All violence, he says, arises in the mind."[13] Quoting a Latin proverb he adds: "*Quod ultimum est in executione, primum est in intentione.* What finally comes out as action was there first in intention."[14] But one can also intend to behave in a manner likely to cause harm without necessarily intending to harm. Instances of negligence that result in harm epitomize this kind of intention.

It should be clear by now that one can do violence psychologically. A father's violent temper can incapacitate a family far more effectively than a father's fist. A mother's sarcasm may injure her children much more irreparably than any physical beating. A suicide bomber's legacy is the fear he or she leaves behind in the survivors. A government's detention of critics and opponents has a much wider harmful and intimidating effect than that of the mere detainment. The physical harm is the more obvious; the psychological harm is the more insidious. The physical harm is the more readily or easily addressed because it is the more obvious, but the psychological harm is the more difficult to identify or overcome in part because it is not always obvious and in part because many people are not disposed to call it violence or recognize it as such.

One reason why psychological violence is more insidious than physical violence is that it is more common. Psychological violence always accompanies physical violence, but physical violence does not always accompany psychological violence. Wars and domestic beatings both cause physical harm to people and their possessions. But accompanying this physical harm is psychological harm. War leaves both civilians and soldiers suffering from post-traumatic stress disorder, as do domestic beatings. But psychological violence can and usually does occur without physical violence. A father's constant criticism or anger toward his children need never be accompanied by a spanking or a physical blow, but the harm done to the child may be serious and irreparable nonetheless.

Furthermore, when physical violence does erupt, and *erupt* is probably the correct term, it erupts because there has been a seething of emotions beneath the surface, emotions that in all likelihood have been generated by one's having suffered from psychological violence. The two young murderers of the so-called trench-coat mafia of Littleton, Colorado, were indeed vicious and psychopathic, but they weren't born that way. They often suffered taunting and neglect, long before they became killers. And this is undoubtedly the case with most instances of doing violence. Even nations, which do not have minds of their own, comprise populations who go to war usually only after having suffered what they regard as indignities or outrages, real or imagined, only after having suffered what could and should be called psychological violence.

But perhaps it is incorrect to label sarcasm and anger as doing violence? Can't someone be aggressive without doing violence? Can't someone be negative or even critically humorous without doing violence? Doesn't this carry matters just a bit too far?

It might. It depends, however, on the sort of sarcasm or anger that is being used, on the context of that sarcasm or the frequency of the anger. It even depends, perhaps, on the "target" of the sarcasm or anger. Is the sarcasm directed toward someone who enjoys engaging in verbal play? Or is it directed against a child whose self-worth is diminished every time she is criticized? Is the anger an occasional outburst, or is it a tool that a father uses to chase others away, as if he were brandishing a knife? Is the military checkpoint simply that, or does it constitute reckless disregard for how it humiliates others?

What separates sarcasm, anger, hostility, assertiveness, and so forth that are *not* instances of doing violence from sarcasm and anger and so on that *are* psychologically violent is the presence either of an intent to diminish someone, to make someone less well off, or of an intent to act in such a way that someone is likely to be diminished or made less well off. Measuring the physical harm of a bullet hole is much easier than measuring the psychological harm of a caustic remark. The bullet hole is more obvious. But a little remark can also have a more damaging effect. Here is an instructive example.

I was once collecting writing assignments in a class. I asked students to pass their papers forward. And after I had collected all the papers one young woman in the class raised her hand and asked if I would mind if she turned her paper in late. I told her to see me after class, and then I turned to the entire class and said, "Let me give you all a word of advice: when you wish to seek an exception to a rule from a professor, always approach the professor privately instead of publicly. It is easier for the professor to make an exception that way." At that point the young woman stood up, burst into tears, and ran from the room. I found her after class and attempted to calm her down, but my words had stung her. Whereas before she had been an attentive and top student in the class, after this event she attended class infrequently, and her grades fell.

Had I done violence to her? I did not think so. My words certainly had a harmful effect on her, but it was not reasonable to expect that those words would have had such an effect. Still, there was a scolding aspect to my remarks. I could have made the same remarks a day later in that very class with the same effect on the class and not the same effect on the particular student. My remarks were in some small degree *aimed* at that woman, helpful though my advice might have been for others.

This example is not meant to point a finger of blame at myself. Nor is it intended to suggest that we should never offer critical advice. It is meant to show that people can be diminished, made less well off, by the subtlest of actions. To avoid doing violence, even well-intentioned people, institutions, communities, and nations must be self-vigilant. Too often we point fingers of blame at others, neglecting our own involve-

Chapter 2

ment, however slight, in a culture in which people do violence to one another regularly through unwitting or negligent actions.

Insofar as doing violence to others is likely to harm them, it is undoubtedly wrong *prima facie*, that is, everything else being equal. There is an obligation not to destroy or harm willfully. This obligation arises from people's ability to recognize the purpose and goals of others. This obligation is not necessarily absolute. But it is an obligation *prima facie*—a presumptive obligation, that is, an obligation not to harm or destroy unless there are overriding reasons to do so. A nation or a person might actually inflict harm on others intentionally (for example, in self-defense or by following orders), but whether or not the act is wrong remains a separate question from whether or not the act is an act of violence. Some acts of violence might be justifiable. [15]

Nonetheless, a major mistake has been to restrict our understanding of violence to physically destructive acts. In so doing we tend to focus more on the effects and less on the harmful intention. Harmful intentions are manifested far more often in acts of psychological abuse than they are in acts of physical abuse. This is partly because psychological violence is always a concomitant of physical violence. People suffer from believing that someone wishes to do them harm—or from knowing that someone has harmed them, or from another's contempt or disregard for them—just as they suffer from physical harm. But harmful intentions are manifested more often in acts of psychological abuse than in physical abuse also because the heart of violence is in the mind of the perpetrator, not in the means by which the intention is carried out nor in the effects of the action. Furthermore, we often perform acts of violence through negligence or omission, by failing to notice the harm that policies, procedures, and habits inflict, perhaps unintentionally, on individuals or groups of people. Some of the voting regulations in the United States, for example, prohibit some people from reaching the polling stations because the hours of voting are restricted to hours when people are at work. In short, not until we begin to recognize the primacy of psychological violence in ourselves and in others, not until we recognize the insidiousness of certain institutional practices, as well, will we be able to address the plague of violent behavior with which we continue to be so concerned. The focus on physical violence hides the psychological and institutional violence that comprise most of the violence from which we all suffer *and that we all perpetrate*. Only heightened sensitivity and awareness of these subtler forms of violence will reduce the more visible physical violence that erupts as a consequence of the less visible, subtler forms in which violence masks itself.

NOTES

1. Taken from a newspaper account summarized by Newton Garver, "What Violence Is," *The Nation* 209 (June 24, 1968): 817–22.

2. Neil Weiner et al., editors, *Violence: Patterns, Causes, and Public Policy* (San Diego, Calif.: Harcourt, Brace, Jovanovich, 1990), xiii.

3. Jerry M. Burger, "Replicating Milgram: Would People Still Obey Today?" *American Psychologist* 64 *(*January 2009), 1–11.

4. Stanley Milgram, "Behavioral Study of Obedience," *Journal of Abnormal and Social Psychology* 67 (1963): 371–78.

5. Robert L. Holmes, *On War and Morality* (Princeton, N.J.: Princeton University Press, 1989) , 42. Holmes also notes three different uses of the term violence: "central, extended, and peripheral uses." Central uses typically refer to the use of physical force; for example: "The bombing of Hiroshima was a violent act." Extended uses of the term typically refer to violations of people or what is sometimes called psychological violence; for example, "She cowered whenever he directed his violent temper toward her." Peripheral uses of the term are typically metaphorical; for example, "The violence of the paint on the canvas stirred up all sorts of emotions in me." These distinctions reveal the wide uses of the term *violence*. See Holmes, *On War and Morality*, 28 –34.

6. E-mail correspondence from Trudy Govier, October 30, 2002.

7. Holmes, *On War and Morality*, 42.

8. Garver, "What Violence Is."

9. See, for example, L. Berkowitz, "The Frustration-Aggression Hypothesis: Examination and Reformulation," *Psychological Bulletin* 106 (1989): 59 –73. And also Govier, as cited above.

10. Michael N. Nagler, *Is There No Other Way? The Search for a Nonviolent Future* (Berkeley, Calif.: Berkeley Hills Books, 2001), 46, quoted from Charlton Lewis and Charles Short, *A Latin Dictionary* (Oxford: Oxford University Press, 1962), under *violare*.

11. Nagler, *Is There No Other Way?*46–47.

12. Nagler, *Is There No Other Way?*47.

13. Nagler, *Is There No Other Way?*47.

14. Nagler, *Is There No Other Way?* 49.

15. Holmes, *On War and Morality*, 37 –38.

Chapter Three

The Myth of Good Guys and Bad Guys

Imagine two men.

One of these men is well off, respected in his community, respected nationally, respected internationally. He is married and a loving father of several children. Nonetheless, he engages somewhat regularly in extramarital affairs. He hides these affairs from his wife and family, but his friends know about them. He continues this behavior year after year. The other man is also well off, in fact, very well off. He, too, is married and the father of several children. Though he could be far wealthier than he is, instead he devotes his efforts to charity for veterans. He visits wounded soldiers, talking with them and bringing them food and chocolates. He visits the families of veterans who have been killed or injured, comforting them and providing them with money and means with which to make a living.

It seems clear which of the two men described above is the better person. Doesn't it? At least, it seems clear until one learns who these two men are. The first person described above, the adulterer, is Martin Luther King, Jr. The FBI placed microphones in King's hotel rooms and captured on tape various sexual liaisons that he had outside of his marriage.[1] The second man described above, the man charitable to veterans and their families, is Osama bin Laden. Prior to the 9/11 attacks Osama bin Laden was well known throughout the Muslim world for his military service and charitable activities in the Afghan war against the Soviet Union.[2]

Suddenly our conclusions about these two men don't seem so clear. Now the images blur a bit.

The point, however, is not that Osama bin Laden is a good guy. Osama bin Laden, directly or indirectly, was responsible for the murder of many innocent people. Those are violent acts . . . and bad. Nor is the point that Martin Luther King, Jr. is a bad guy. Although his adultery is not admirable, his life was also filled with many admirable deeds. No, these stories offer other lessons: first, that despite very strong tendencies to view individuals as either good or bad, despite a cultural myth that some people are the personification of good and others the personification of evil, we err in thinking so. And second, when we persist in such typecasting, we ourselves do violence to those we typecast, and we invite violence on the part of others because our use of such labels helps to condone the violence that people wish to perpetrate against those who are considered bad.

THE MYTH AT WORK

The myth that there are good people and bad people operates on several levels. As the example above shows, it is used in ways that justify our classification of individuals as good or evil. But it is also used to justify our classification of *groups* of people—ethnic groups, nation-states, races—as good or evil. And it also underlies the widely held view that people are by nature evil or aggressive and regularly in need of having that evil or aggression contained. Here are some examples of the first variant of the myth of good guys and bad guys, the first from a civilian observer in Baghdad in 2005:

> On a recent trip north I happened to be in a queue of traffic at a checkpoint outside Mosul when a suicide car bomb exploded some meters ahead of us. A short time later a U.S. soldier, with whom I was talking at the bomb site, asked me "Does anyone, other than the bad guys, know you are coming?" He saw the state of affairs in Iraq as a good guy/bad guy situation, the U.S. of course being the "good guys."

The civilian observer continues:

> The targeting of foreigners in Iraq, or anyone associated with them, is yet another example of this oversimplification: foreigners = bad. Similarly, militants target people because they are Christian (unbelievers) or

because they are Sunni or Shi'a (not true believers)—believer/unbeliever being the religious extremist's good guy/bad guy.[3]

The attitude summarized by this civilian observer was confirmed for me on an airplane trip I took, also in 2005, when I happened to sit next to an infantryman who was about to return for a second tour of duty in war-torn Iraq. I asked him about the kinds of action he had seen and how long he felt the war was likely to continue. He told me that he had been in several long battles in which entire towns were leveled, in which he and his comrades went from house to house, killing anyone left in the towns. He said that there were "a bunch of assholes" there, and it would probably take five or six years before we could "get rid of them all." I asked him if there weren't ordinary families there who just wanted to conduct their lives like families everywhere, and he said, "Oh, sure. Don't get me wrong. There are a lot of good people there. But it's going to take a while to get rid of the assholes."

Leaders of extremist groups are certainly inclined toward this sort of thinking, but most of us do not regard ordinary infantrymen as extremists. Unfortunately, all of us, including leaders of nations, are victims and perpetrators of this black-and-white thinking. Here is George W. Bush in remarks to the Warsaw Conference, November 6, 2001:

> Given the means, our enemies would be a threat to every nation and eventually to civilization itself. So we're determined to fight this evil, and fight until we're rid of it. We will not wait for the authors of mass murder to gain the weapons of mass destruction. We act now, because we must lift this dark threat from our age and save generations to come.[4]

And here is Osama bin Laden, the focus of George W. Bush's remarks in 2001, expressing very similar sentiments in a broadcast on Doha Al-Jazirah Satellite Channel Television on January 4, 2004:

> They want to dictate democracy and Americanize our culture through their jet bombers. Therefore, what is yet to come is even more malicious and devilish. The occupation of Iraq is a link in the Zionist-Crusader chain of evil. Then comes the full occupation of the rest of the Gulf states to set the stage for controlling and dominating the whole world. . . . There can be no dialogue with the occupiers except with weapons.[5]

There is nothing new about such language, nothing new about this myth. People invoke this myth whenever they are in need of justifying violent action or whenever they are inclined to incite others to violent action.

Here are three quotations from Adolf Hitler, the first two from *Mein Kampf*, the third from a speech given to the Reichstag on May 4, 1941:

- The personification of the devil as the symbol of all evil assumes the living shape of the Jew.[6]
- It is the inexorable Jew who struggles for his domination over the nations. No nation can remove this hand from its throat except by the sword. . . . Such a process is and remains a bloody one.[7]
- The man behind this fanatical and diabolical plan to bring about war at whatever cost was Mr. Churchill.[8]

The language then, too, was apocalyptic, and it was not unique to Hitler. Here is Winston Churchill, speaking *a year earlier* than Hitler's Reichstag speech, on May 13, 1940:

> You ask, what is our policy? I say it is to wage war by land, sea, and air. War with all our might and with all the strength God has given us, and to wage war against a monstrous tyranny never surpassed in the dark and lamentable catalogue of human crime. That is our policy.[9]

Each of the people quoted above—Bush, bin Laden, Hitler, and Churchill—identifies his opponents as evil, devilish, or monstrous enemies. Each speaks of the necessity of ridding the world of these enemies. Each encourages actions that will most certainly kill innocent people. But these sentiments are not unique to politics: variants of this myth are also at work at the individual level, and in religion and science as well.

The temptation is strong to resist the comparisons above. After all, Winston Churchill was not Hitler, and bin Laden was not Bush. But the urge to resist the comparisons is precisely the problem. Churchill wasn't urging merely that *Hitler* be removed from power or killed: he was urging war on all of Germany, urging, implicitly, that millions of German citizens, not much different from the Britons whom Churchill represented, be targeted and killed. Bush was urging not merely that bin Laden be captured or killed but urging two months later in his 2002 State of the Union address that the fight be taken to Iraq, North Korea, and Iran, if necessary. Like Churchill, he was implicitly recommending that we kill significant numbers of their populations and destroy their infrastructures because Iraq, Iran, and North Korea constituted an "axis of evil."[10] We now know—and many were telling the United States in 2001—that the people of Iraq and Afghanistan were not the source of the problem.

Iraq had nothing to do with the 9/11 attacks, and while bin Laden had camps in Afghanistan, no Afghans were among the suicide bombers. According to the U.S. 9/11 Commission Report, the suicide bombers came primarily from Saudi Arabia, as did planners of the attack, and though the governments of Afghanistan, Saudi Arabia, and Iran allowed those involved in the attacks to travel relatively freely through their countries, the commission concluded that the governments of those countries knew nothing about the plan itself.[11] And even if they had, the United States would not have been warranted in attacking entire countries as it did. A major impetus for violence on a grand scale is the painting of an entire population as evil because of the words or actions of a few.

Hitler, Churchill, bin Laden, Bush, and many other leaders are equally guilty of such artistry, guilty of rousing populations that are capable of being roused to commit mass murder in the name of justice or national security. The Bryce Commission, for example, was established in England near the beginning of World War I.

> Lord Bryce and several attorneys documented atrocities committed by German soldiers against Belgians: the rape of young women in public, the cutting off of women's breasts, the bayoneting of young children. These atrocities, needless to say, outraged the British public and helped to draw Britain into the war. The stories were repeated in the U.S. press, and thus began decades of German-bashing. The only problem is that the stories were false. American reporters traveling with the German army saw no evidence of these atrocities. Efforts to find even a single refugee who witnessed an atrocity met with no success. The Bryce Commission report was thoroughly discredited after the war, but the damage had been done long before by the press, among others. An entire population had been painted as evil, and an entire war justified on the grounds of such claims.[12]

Most of us can remember our own sense of outrage when a teacher would punish an entire class for the misbehavior of one or two students, who themselves were not an axis of evil but simply individuals acting out on occasion. When a government engages in such practices, it's called collective punishment, and it is a violation of international law. But leaders bent on going to war rouse entire populations, people like you and me, to make exactly these sorts of judgments and to go to war on the basis of such judgments.

The source of the problem, as argued above, is the readiness of many people—the country or region doesn't matter, those in the Middle East, for example, or many in the United States as well, for example—to believe that people can be divided neatly into two groups, the good and the bad. And once that division is made, it is truly a very small step to conclude that the bad must be eradicated or killed, and in large numbers if necessary. But the average German in 1937 was not that much different than the average Briton in 1937. Nor was the average Afghan or Iraqi that much different—except in economic terms—than the average American. Almost everyone in every country at any time wants little more than to live his or her life with family and friends, enjoying free time and conversation, falling in love, having a family. The numbers of individuals who can be classified as inherently evil are an infinitesimally small percentage of any population. But the numbers of people who can be roused by demagogues to believe that others are evil are virtually uncountable because they include almost all of humankind.

Within almost every religious denomination one can find extremists who regard anyone not of their religion as somehow lacking. This is true of Christians, Jews, Muslims, and Hindus, among others. While the mainstream proponents within each religion may decry the views of such extremists, many others admire and support them. I have heard Jews proclaim that all Palestinians are bad. I've heard Christians describe non-Christians as hopelessly lost souls. In 2002 Muslims and Hindus lashed out in religious violence against each other in Gujarat province in India, Gandhi's home province, leaving hundreds of Hindus and hundreds of Muslims dead.[13]

But even many people outside of any religious tradition have a similar myth in place: they see human beings as innately aggressive and inclined toward violence. Although recent scientific theories on aggression temper such claims, early theories about aggression, most notably those of Sigmund Freud and Konrad Lorenz, promoted such a view. Among non-scientists, it is almost a platitude that people are innately aggressive. And if we are all innately aggressive, then, some suggest, we all need to be properly channeled—by operant conditioning, by genetic engineering, by drugs, by therapy, by the threat of punishment. And the most evil among us, those who never learned to channel their aggression productively, so the myth continues, must be "eliminated"—killed.

The good guy/bad guy dichotomy is thus apocalyptic, suggesting that the salvation of the world or the redemption of oneself lies in the elimination of "the other." One can find this dichotomy in almost every bitter contest, no matter how large or small.

I participated once in a parade to "support the troops." Our peace group, opposed to the war at that time, carried signs urging that the government improve war veterans' benefits, support soldier's families, and bring the troops home now. As we turned the corner at the end of the parade, one veteran, not with our group, stood on the side of the road, tossing pebbles and yelling insults at us. I walked over to him to let him know that some of the people at whom he was throwing pebbles and insults were themselves veterans of war and people from war veterans' families. However, before I could open my mouth he yelled, "Don't even fucking talk to me! I don't want to hear what you have to say." His voice was at a level aimed at drowning out anything I might say to him. But eventually, he ran out of things to yell, and when he halted momentarily, I squeezed in the few words that I had come over to say, let him know that among those at whom he was hurling his insults and his little stones were some veterans. He replied, "Well, they aren't *good* veterans." For him, too, even the world of veterans was divided into good veterans and bad veterans.

So we paint people as evil, and they thus become tarnished with evil and we become directed by the portrait. During wartime, enemies come to regard each other as evil incarnate, and the use of language by the leaders of nations reflects that. Thus, through U.S. eyes, Hitler was evil, and so were the "Japs." Later, the Soviet Union was branded an evil empire by Ronald Reagan. More recently, as noted earlier, George W. Bush branded Saddam Hussein as evil, and Iran and North Korea, too. Through the eyes of Al-Qaeda, the United States is evil. And through the eyes of the Nazis, the Jews were evil. Letters to the editor in the United States in the years following the 2001 attacks on the Pentagon and the World Trade Center ignored the Crusades and at least five hundred years of Christian anti-Semitism and branded Islam as a murderous religion. When we paint our opponents as evil, whether along individual, ethnic, national, or religious lines, we act intentionally in a way likely to cause harm. We do violence to our opponents and create an atmosphere that condones others, often ourselves, who would harm them.

DECONSTRUCTING THE MYTH

But this myth—the notion that some of us are good and some of us are bad, or that all of us are innately bad because we are innately aggressive—is both false and unhelpful.

Anyone who thinks about this honestly knows it is so. Each of us has done good, and each of us has done bad. Although one's image in the world may be that of a good person or that of a bad person, in reality no one is purely good or purely evil. The sooner we come to terms with this fact, the sooner we can erase the myth that there are good people and bad people. Certainly some people do far more good than bad, and certainly some people do far more bad than good, and while it might be convenient to refer to such people as good or bad, respectively, such labels increase rather than diminish the levels of violence in the world.[14]

In the first place, the use of such labels is itself a violent act. It does violence to the truth of the matter, which is that probably no one is entirely good or entirely bad. It does violence to the person to whom we attach the label. In the case of people we label as good, it forces them to live up to an image that no one can reasonably be expected to live up to, an image of perfection. In the case of people we label as bad, it lets them know that there is no way they can ever redeem themselves, lets them know that, in our eyes, they are finished as human beings with any worth.

This labeling is perhaps most evident in schools, where children are often labeled as good or bad by their peers and even by teachers. I once taught in public schools, and it was remarkable to me how many of the teachers who had been there for years had labeled students as bad or good simply because they came from certain families, simply because they had had an older brother or sister who had been "bad" or "good." The damage done to siblings by this sort of labeling is more than unfair; it is itself a violent act that harms students by disposing others to act differently toward them than they otherwise might.

In the second place, the use of such labels serves as a justification or excuse for our own violent behavior. This is so because whenever anyone invokes the myth, it is always to assign the label of "bad" or "evil" to the other, never to oneself. The bad guys are never "us," whoever "us" happens to be. The bad guys are always the other guys. We're always the "good guys." Rare indeed are the persons or nations who call themselves evil. By calling other persons "bad" or "evil," we are able to relegate them to some status lower than ours, and we are thereby able to justify treating them differently than we would treat "good people."

Labeling others as inherently bad or evil excuses us from having to treat them as we might treat ourselves. It constitutes permission to treat them differently, to deny them privileges or rights that so-called good people have. Furthermore, as the quotations above have shown, even those who regard themselves as "good" are regarded as "evil" by others. It doesn't matter whether one party actually is good and the other party bad: as long as each party regards itself as good and the other party as bad, every party will be regarded by some party as bad, as deserving of disruption, punishment, elimination, death.

The truth of the matter, again, is that we are each good *and* bad, each capable of harming and helping others. We are innately aggressive *and* innately compassionate and loving. Ultimately, neither civilization nor religion inclines a person to help or to harm others, to live in right relations. Rather, people make those choices for themselves, finding in a religion or a civilization the support for choices that they have already made.[15] Civilization and religion have both been known to help people make good choices, but they have also both been known to incite people to make bad choices.

OVERCOMING THE MYTH

We all have the potential to do good and to do bad. We all have the potential to do violence and to refrain from doing violence. I, myself, for example, am committed to nonviolence. I am opposed to violence in all of its forms. I believe that it is a duty to avoid resorting to violence. I believe that when I am struck, psychologically or physically, I must do all I can to overcome the impulse to strike back. I *have* the impulse to strike back, but I work to resist that impulse. Nonetheless, I know that there are circumstances under which I would resort to violence. I would, for example, probably do whatever I could do or must do in order to stop someone who was an immediate threat to my own life or the life of my children or wife. And so would most of us.

Anyone who denies their potential to treat others violently is either a
saint or a liar.

A more common form of violence is the lie. Almost all of us lie. We
lie to our spouses, our children, our friends, that they look good or
performed well because we don't want to hurt their feelings. We steer a
conversation away from a focus on a truth that might be hurtful or
damaging to a relationship. We lie when we are afraid that telling the
truth will harm us. What is violent about the lies we all tell?

Gandhi equated God with Truth. He said that God is Truth and
Truth is God. The Hindi word for truth is *satya*, and the root of that
word, *sat*, means being or existence. Gandhi believed that each being in
the universe, not just human beings, not just all animal and plant life,
but all beings, has a piece of the truth, and that if we destroy being, we
destroy truth. Gandhi also believed that it was impossible to live without wreaking destruction of some kind or another but that it was incum-
bent upon us to minimize violence as much as is in our power.

In this respect the views of Albert Schweitzer are remarkably similar though Schweitzer restricted himself more explicitly to speaking of
all life rather than all beings, living or not. Schweitzer said, "I am life
that wants to live in the midst of other life that wants to live. A thinking
man feels compelled to approach all life with the same reverence he has
for his own."[16]

A lie, then, not only shows a lack of reverence toward others, reverence that one has for one's own life. It also denies what is real, what is
true. To the extent that others believe one's lies, one does them harm.
One helps to create in them a picture of the world that is not true, and
insofar as others act upon this picture of the universe, they run risks that
they might not otherwise take if they knew the truth. And, as mentioned
earlier, a lie forces the liar to become two personalities, the one who
must keep up the façade and the one who continues to act within the
façade.

Almost all of us lie, often in the belief that a white lie, a misleading
remark, or an out-and-out deception is less hurtful than the truth. But
the lie is less hurtful only if the truth is never discovered. If discovered,
the lie becomes even more hurtful than the truth would have been.

Martin Luther King Jr., Mahatma Gandhi, and Jesus of Nazareth all
insisted that we love our enemies. And to most of us that seems absurd.
An enemy is someone you hate, not someone you love. But Gandhi
explained: we may hate what our enemies *do*, but we may not hate
them for what they *are*. For we are all quite similar. In the same

circumstances you and I might behave very much like our enemies. People's tendencies to lie, people's willingness to do violence to others under orders, as the summary of Milgram's experiments showed in the previous chapter, also help to establish this point—that we are all very likely under the right circumstances to behave very much like our enemies.

Thus we have a responsibility to behave toward all others with a respect for their capacity to do good and an appreciation of their capacity to do evil. When we insult others, when we regard them as incapable of goodness, we do violence to them. We forget that they, too, are part of a community, that they have mothers and fathers who love them, children whom they love, dreams quite like ours that they wish to fulfill.

I once mediated a dispute between a school bus driver and a woman on her route. The bus driver claimed that this woman on her route owned a dog that would attack children as they stepped off the school bus. The woman on the route denied that claim. The two women, seated together in the mediation room, would not look at each other. Each was so angry with the other that each refused to speak directly to the other. They directed their words toward me. Finally the woman on the bus route said, "I have a dog like the one she described. But he doesn't attack the children. There is another dog on the street that is doing that." The bus driver said to me, "See how she lies?" Then the other woman replied, "I've had the dog ever since my husband, Gary, died, and he has never attacked children." At this point, suddenly the bus driver exclaimed, "Gary *died*?!" Until that moment I hadn't known the women even knew each other. It turned out that they used to play cards together. Whatever enmity had arisen between them over the years was eliminated when the bus driver learned of the death of the dog owner's husband. Suddenly Gary's wife became a human being again in the eyes of the bus driver. Within minutes they settled the conflict because the bus driver became willing to believe Gary's wife.

This story shows that often we are able to settle disputes simply by acknowledging the humanity of our opponents, simply by acknowledging that one's opponent is a lot like us, capable of doing good if given the chance, capable of doing bad if nothing we do will change people's opinion of us. You and I contribute to violence because all too often we do not realize that we have stopped treating our opponents with the recognition or dignity they deserve, all too often we have stopped recognizing that our opponents have the same potentials for good and bad that we have.

The myth prevents us from achieving this recognition.

The other variant of this myth, that people are by nature aggressive or violent and that we must recognize this aggressiveness when we develop policies or patterns of behavior, neglects other important truths about human beings. Hints of these truths can be found in a Cherokee legend.

> An old Cherokee is teaching his grandson about life. "A fight is going on inside me," he said to the boy.
>
> "It is a terrible fight and it is between two wolves. One is evil—he is anger, envy, sorrow, regret, greed, arrogance, self-pity, guilt, resentment, inferiority, lies, false pride, superiority, and ego." He continued, "The other is good—he is joy, peace, love, hope, serenity, humility, kindness, benevolence, empathy, generosity, truth, compassion, and faith. The same fight is going on inside you—and inside every other person, too."
>
> The grandson thought about it for a minute and then asked his grandfather, "Which wolf will win?"
>
> The old Cherokee simply replied, "The one you feed." [17]

More than any other creatures on earth, we people have the capacity to alter our environments. We also have a pretty good idea about what sorts of environmental stimuli promote and retard aggressive and violent tendencies in human beings and other animals. Thus, whether or not we are by nature aggressive or violent, we have the ability—and know that we have the ability—to curb dramatically our own aggressive or violent tendencies. To view people as bad because they are of the wrong religion, or because they are uncivilized, or because they are aggressive, is itself a violent posture that ignores our capabilities to become less violent, ignores our tendencies for love and compassion, tendencies at least as "innate" as aggression.

Like other animals, people often react violently when forced into a corner. But unlike other animals, people have the capacity to anticipate the future, to plan for it, to alter it, to prevent boxing others into corners. Unfortunately, more often than not, we do behave as other animals. We fail to look far enough into the future to see the effects of our own actions. For instance, the U.S. military, indeed, the militaries of all countries, for example, seek to minimize harm to citizens of their own countries. Nations spend tremendous amounts of money to achieve security at home through military power. But we don't look deeply enough at the effects of this. Specifically, the governments of the world spend approximately $1,100 per student per year. However, the governments of the world spend approximately thirty times that amount per soldier per year: $36,000 per soldier per year.[18] More recent statistics reveal that in recent years the United States spent somewhat less than ten thousand dollars per student per year[19] but several hundred thousand dollars per soldier per year.[20]

These statistics suggest strongly that the teenagers of the world know better how to kill than how to read. What might they know better if we reversed those figures? If we spent $30,000 per student per year and $1,100 per soldier per year? Which wolf shall we feed?

Television and movies also lead one to believe that violent criminals are different kinds of people than you and me. Television shows and movies—especially the early Disney cartoon movies—make quite evident who is "the bad guy." In the Disney cartoons, for many years, the "bad guy" was almost always a woman, often a single woman: the jealous Queen in *Snow White*, the stepmother in *Cinderella*, Ursula in *The Little Mermaid*, the wicked fairy in *Sleeping Beauty*. There are some nasty men, too: Captain Hook in *Peter Pan*, some of the characters in *Pinocchio*. And the more recent cartoons have been more balanced: In *Beauty and the Beast*, for example, Belle is pitted against a boorish brute. But it remains true that in all these movies the problems in the world are attributed to the malice of a single person (and perhaps some accomplices) incapable of anything but evil. Somehow it's never that easy in real life. We're never quite sure of our opponents—never quite as sure who they are or what their motives are.

To the extent that these attitudes of "us-as-good" and "them-as-evil" become a part of our orientation, we choose to regard people who are essentially like ourselves as less than human, providing ourselves and others with a justification for acting in ways that we otherwise would not act, for acting in ways that most definitely harm other people. Of course, "they" are doing the same thing. The behaviors become a form of violence, an intent to act in ways that harm another, and these behaviors spiral upward. We become convinced that it is wiser to spend money on arms rather than education, on training people to destroy communities instead of build them.

In short, the willingness to develop our physical and social environments to promote rather than retard aggression and violence is also a form of violence. The willingness to view others as less than human, as

evil, as people inherently different from ourselves, is a form of violence. These behaviors and attitudes take a psychological and sometimes a physical toll on both perpetrators and victims. These behaviors
and attitudes are a myth that we should discard. If we persist in the
myth, we shall persist in the violence that it helps support.

NOTES

1. Ralph David Abernathy, *And the Walls Came Tumbling Down* (New York: Harper & Row, 1989).
2. Jason Burke, "The Making of the World's Most Wanted Man," *The Observer*,
October 28, 2001, http://www.guardian.co.uk/news/2001/oct/28/world.terrorism (accessed on June 9, 2009). Burke writes of bin Laden:

> Journalists in Pakistan at the beginning of the Eighties remember hearing
> stories about the "Saudi sheikh" who would visit wounded fighters in the
> university town's clinics, dispensing cashew nuts and chocolates. The man
> would note their names and addresses and soon a generous cheque would
> arrive at their family home. Such generosity—perhaps learnt from his father
> with his wad of notes for the poor—is something that almost all who have
> fought for or alongside bin Laden mention.
>   Some—such as one former al-Qaeda member interviewed by The Ob-
> server in Algeria—speak of $1,500 donations for marriages, others talk of
> cash doled out for shoes or watches or needy relatives. His followers say
> that such gifts bind them to their emir as effectively as the bayat or oath that
> many of them swear.

3. Jan Benvie, "Iraq Reflection: The Good, the Bad and the Innocent," posted August 23, 2005, http://groups.yahoo.com/group/cpt_iraq/message/977 (accessed August
31, 2005).
4. George W. Bush, remarks before the Warsaw Conference on Combating Terrorism, November 6, 2001, http://www.washington.polemb.net/sites/embassy_post//
Numer4/Numer4_Conference.htm (accessed on June 14, 2009).
5. "Full text: 'Bin Laden' Tape," *BBC News*, January 4, 2004, http://news.bbc.co.
uk/2/hi/middle_east/3368957.stm (accessed on May 28, 2012).
6. Adolf Hitler, *Mein Kampf*, vol. 1: A Reckoning, chapter 11: "Nation and Race,"
http://www.hitler.org/writings/Mein_Kampf/mkv1ch11.html (accessed on January 7,
2012).
7. Hitler, *Mein Kampf*, vol. 2: The National Socialist Movement, chapter 14: "Eastern Orientation or Eastern Policy," http://www.hitler.org/writings/Mein_Kampf/
mkv2ch14.html (accessed on January 7, 2012).
8. Adolf Hitler, speech in the Reichstag on May 4, 1941, http://www.hitler.org/
speeches/05-04-41.html (accessed on June 15, 2009).
9. Winston Churchill, "Blood, Toil, Tears and Sweat," first speech to the House of
Commons, May 13, 1940, Internet Modern History Sourcebook, http://www.fordham.
edu/halsall/mod/churchill-blood.html (accessed on June 15, 2009).
10. George W. Bush, State of the Union Address, January 29, 2002, Miller Center,
University of Virginia, http://millercenter.org/president/speeches/detail/4540 (accessed
on June 8. 2012).

11. "The Attack Looms," in *The 9/11 Commission Report* (Washington, D.C.: Executive Agency Publications, U.S. Government Printing Office, July 22, 2004), 215–53.

12. Taken from History News Network, The Center for History and New Media at George Mason University, June 9, 2003, http://hnn.us/articles/printfriendly/1489.html (accessed June 2, 2005), as cited in Barry L. Gan, "Pressed Into War," *Peace Review* 17 (Winter 2005): 344–45.

13. "Top BJP Man Seeks Gujarat Probe," *BBC News*, May 13, 2005, http://news.bbc.co.uk/2/hi/south_asia/4543177.stm (accessed on June 8, 2012).

14. See Robert L. Holmes, "Understanding Evil from the Perspective of Nonviolence," *The Acorn* 14, no. 1 (Winter–Spring 2010): 5–13.

15. See Jean-Paul Sartre's essay "Existentialism is a Humanism."

16. Excerpts from "Albert Schweitzer Speaks Out," A Year Book Special Report from the 1964 World Book Year Book (Chicago: Field Enterprises Educational Corporation, 1964), as cited in *Nonviolence in Theory and Practice*, ed. Robert L. Holmes and Barry L. Gan (Long Grove, Ill.: Waveland Press, 2012), 315.

17. "Two Wolves," First People—The Legends, http://www.firstpeople.us/FP-Html-Legends/TwoWolves-Cherokee.html (accessed on May 28, 2012).

18. Ruth Leger Sivard, *World Military and Social Expenditures 1991* (Washington, D.C.: World Priorities, 1991), 26.

19. U.S. Department of Education, Institute of Education Sciences, "Revenue and Expenditures for Public Elementary and Secondary Education, School Year 2002–03," http://nces.ed.gov/ccd/pubs/npefs03/findings.asp (accessed on June 15, 2009).

20. "U.S. Spends More per Soldier than Ever Before," MSNBC, February 16, 2005, http://www.msnbc.msn.com/id/6978975/ (accessed on May 28, 2012).

Chapter Four

The Myth of Necessary Violence

The notion that we are good people and that there are bad people out to "get us"—be they our bosses, our rivals, our economic competitors, or other nations—often leads us to believe that in order to prevent the violence that "they" would do to us, we must sometimes resort to violence ourselves. But anyone who thinks even briefly about the idea that violence is sometimes necessary to prevent violence will realize that, on its face, the statement is a contradiction in terms. Imagine a few other statements of the same form:

- Eating is sometimes necessary to prevent eating.
- Talking is sometimes necessary to prevent talking.
- Illness is sometimes necessary to prevent illness.

Similarly, one does not prevent violence by using it. My use of violence *guarantees* the continuance of violence simply because I am, myself, using it. Thus, on the face of it, these statements are absurd. One does not prevent oneself from eating by eating, nor does one put an end to talking by talking, or put an end to illness by illness.

A MORE CHARITABLE INTERPRETATION

However, the last analogy—that illness is sometimes necessary to prevent illness—is instructive. Sometimes one *does* prevent future illness through the use of vaccinations. And vaccinations are usually mild or "dead" forms of the causative agent of the illness. So sometimes one does put an end to a more severe illness, or prevent a more severe illness, by submitting oneself earlier on to a milder form of the illness.

Similarly, sometimes one talks to prevent talking. A teacher, seeking classroom quiet, will often ask students to stop talking. To do so, the teacher must himself talk. And sometimes, too, one eats a little throughout the day to prevent oneself from gorging later.

So when we say that sometimes we must use violence to prevent violence, we typically mean that it is sometimes necessary to use some violence now if we wish to prevent other, greater violence in the future. Nonetheless, before examining this myth in detail, it is crucial to realize what it ultimately means: it means that we believe that *it is sometimes necessary, perhaps even desirable, to perpetrate the very thing we are trying to prevent, to cause harm or injustice to others, sometimes even innocent others*, in the belief that we are preventing greater harm or injustice from occurring.

More specifically, what we usually mean is that our own use of violence is necessary, desirable, or justifiable to prevent *another's* use of violence, or that my use of a little violence now will prevent another's use of greater violence later. This other person or party is frequently a "bad guy," almost always someone "evil" in nature. These sorts of reasons are offered virtually every time a person, an institution, or a nation engages in violence. Consider three examples: the U.S. entry into World War I, the Vietnam War, and the war in Iraq.

THE DIFFICULTY WITH THE CHARITABLE INTERPRETATION

The United States was explicitly neutral during the first few years of World War I. U.S. companies sold armaments to any party in the war that paid for them, and the U.S. government did not stand in the way of such sales. But as the British naval blockade of Germany tightened, most U.S. war supplies reached only England, not Germany. So, in practice, Germany applied this principle: if we use a little violence now, we'll prevent more violence later. German agents began blowing up shipments of U.S. war supplies, sometimes in New York ports, sometimes on the high seas. The most egregious instance of this occurred in May 1915, when a German submarine sank the *Lusitania*, a passenger ship allegedly carrying war supplies. This incident, along with several others, helped to propel the United States into World War I against Germany. Germany's intention to use a little violence now to prevent more violence later backfired. But one could also argue that the U.S. sale of war supplies was itself a violent act that backfired.

U.S. involvement in Vietnam is another example of this principle at work—and backfiring. Slowly, beginning in the 1950s and escalating somewhat in the early 1960s and then dramatically in the mid- to late 1960s, the United States attempted to use a little violence to halt what it thought would become a "domino effect": the violent spread of communism if South Vietnam fell to Communist control. By the mid-1970s more than fifty thousand American lives and millions of Vietnamese lives had been lost, South Vietnam had fallen to Communist control, and the domino effect never occurred. The initial violence, intended to minimize later violence, had the opposite effect, especially because it did not prevent the establishment of a Communist government throughout Vietnam, the establishment of which, in fact, did *not* lead to a domino effect.

Again, the purported aims of the United States in attacking Iraq in 2003 were several, and they kept changing. Initially the aim was to eliminate stockpiles of weapons of mass destruction, none of which actually existed. Subsequently the aim was to remove from power a dictator, Saddam Hussein, who had killed many of his own citizens. But the death and destruction in Iraq since the removal of Saddam Hussein has been far worse than anything seen during the time he was leader. The violence that the United States perpetrated, initially in the first Gulf War and then in what has become known as the Iraq War, unleashed much death and destruction over two decades. Specific figures have never been determined; estimates range from one hundred thousand to more than one million. Is this more than would have died had Saddam Hussein remained in power? No one can say. But the real question, a question that will be pursued and answered in the second part of this book, is whether a third alternative, a nonviolent alternative, would have resulted in fewer deaths and less destruction. The answer is almost certainly a resounding yes.

THE PRACTICAL RELEVANCE OF MEANS TO ENDS

Almost all people agree on the ends of social and political activity. Virtually every one of us seeks a peaceful home, a peaceful community, a peaceful nation, a peaceful world. We disagree over the *means* one pursues in seeking peace. This disagreement over means is what distinguishes those who genuinely desire peace from those who do not.

The insight has been driven home to me by two sets of incidents in recent years. Occasionally I attend synagogue for family events. I've noticed in several synagogues across the country that an important prayer in various prayer books is now translated differently than it had been in years past. Specifically, the translation of a very famous line from Isaiah has been changed. Each week, one of the Sabbath prayers that I had uttered and heard as a teen had been:

> *Lo yiseh goy el goy herev, v'lo yl-medu od ml-hamah.*

In previous years and throughout many translations, these clauses had been translated as follows:

> Nation shall not lift up sword against nation.
> Neither shall men learn war anymore.

But though the Hebrew remains unchanged in the prayer book, the English translation has changed. It now reads:

> Nation shall not lift up sword against nation.
> Neither shall men experience war any more.

"That's curious," I thought. In the original Hebrew the idea was that paradise would be a place where people would not *learn* war anymore. But now the idea has shifted from a world in which nations would not practice war to a world in which nations would not *suffer* war.

I approached rabbis at a couple of these synagogues and asked about this change. I asked whether the Hebrew word *yl-medu* meant "learn" or "experience." I knew what it meant, and so did they. It means "learn." It does not mean "experience." But they made excuses for the translation.

And it was clear to me, at least, why such a translation in an American prayer book had been altered. Israel and the United States both spend a great deal of money, time, and effort in *learning* war. Both nations have turned away from the paradise in which people have ceased to learn and practice war. With many alleged justifications, both nations have incorporated the practice of war and the development of armaments into the fabric of their societies.

The wishes of both nations are that neither of them experience war in their own territories. Neither wishes to suffer war, but both are willing to learn it. Both are willing to learn war—and practice it—in the mistaken view that by doing so they will not suffer it. But the Bible strongly suggests that paradise is the circumstance that obtains, not when nations suffer war no more, but when they *learn* it no more.

Many think otherwise. Many agree with the myth that it is often necessary to use violence to prevent harm to innocent people. In 2006 I heard Archbishop Celestino Migliore speak at the annual conference of the Peace and Justice Studies Association. Migliore was the Pope's representative to the UN, and though I shouldn't have been surprised, I was surprised to hear some of his remarks. When asked whether the Church would condone the use of violence in some circumstances, he said that it would be wrong sometimes to turn the other cheek. I was curious to see how he would explain this since it contradicts what Jesus says in the Beatitudes, and he obliged me by trotting out the following worn example: Imagine a person carrying a baby, assaulted by a third person. Should the person charged with the care of the baby turn the other cheek? No, said the Archbishop, not if it means that the baby would be assaulted—because one has an obligation to protect innocent third parties.

In the first place, one can't know that the violence we're trying to prevent would ever occur. The truth is that people are often needlessly alarmed. As Fisher and Ury write in their book *Getting to Yes*, we should not deduce other people's intentions from our fears.[1] In 2003 the United States feared that Saddam Hussein had weapons of mass destruction, and so it initiated what it called a pre-emptive war. As it turned out, there was nothing to pre-empt.

In the second place, when we use violence to prevent violence, we cannot know in advance that the violence we use will in fact succeed in preventing other violence. Germany counted on its attacks on arms shipments in World War I to reduce the harm that could be inflicted upon it. The United States believed, apparently wrongly, that interventions in Vietnam and in Iraq would prevent greater harm in the long run. Usually at least one side loses in every violent conflict, and sometimes both or all sides lose, but parties do not enter conflicts with an expectation of losing. So at least one party to each conflict usually engages in a mistaken judgment by concluding that they will suffer less by engaging in violence than if they do not.

Moreover, and third, even if the violence that one hoped to prevent does not occur, one cannot conclude that one has succeeded. The Gulf War certainly succeeded in turning Iraq out of Kuwait, but did it succeed in keeping Iraq from attacking Saudi Arabia as was claimed? In the absence of any information suggesting so, no one can know that Iraq would have invaded Saudi Arabia had the Gulf War not been perpetrated. When we use violence to prevent violence that hasn't yet occurred, we have no way of knowing that the violence we aimed to prevent would *have* occurred.

Violence that hasn't yet occurred is thus used as a justification for violence itself.

Fourth, however, sometimes violence or injustice is already under way, and we adopt violence to prevent further violence. But again, the reality of any of these situations is that we do not know that the violence that we adopt as a response to violence will result in less harm than might otherwise have occurred. Let's consider a few examples.

World War II resulted in approximately fifty to sixty million deaths of civilians and combatants. The common wisdom is that had people not resisted Hitler, even more would have died, but such a claim is highly suspect. Denmark, which surrendered to Germany on the first day of Germany's invasion, lost fewer civilians and combatants than any other country involved in the war, a total of approximately four thousand people. But Danish resistance bogged down the Nazis, and the Danes managed to move to safety all but a handful of all Jews living in their country.[2]

One might argue that the Danes were able to do this because so many other nations were fighting militarily against Germany at the time. But if every nation in Europe had resisted Germany as the Danes did, Germany would not have been able to rule effectively. Any conquering nation requires the support of a substantial portion of the population of the territories it inhabits. If a conquered nation refuses to collaborate, as the Danes refused, the occupying nation is stymied, even more if every occupied nation resists. The success—partial or otherwise—of Germany's invasion of other countries often depended upon the cooperation of large numbers of residents of the countries under occupation as evidenced, for example, by the Vichy government in France.

The costs of the American Civil War are still felt today, and there are many reasons to think that it was a war best not fought at all. In the first place, historians agree that slavery in the South probably would have ended by 1900, anyway. In the second place, many leaders of the antislavery movement opposed the Civil War, believing it unnecessary. Prominent among them, but only one example, was Lucretia Mott, who had dedicated much of her life to ending slavery. Third, prior to the

Civil War many northern states had permitted slavery themselves and had done away with it in the decades leading up to the Civil War. Finally, even if the war was fought primarily to preserve the Union, it is by no means clear that the United States or the world is better off because Lincoln kept the North and the South under a single flag. But six hundred thousand people died as a result of that war, and the bitterness and the legacy of a forced end to slavery engendered by that war continues 150 years later.

These examples are meant to show that the value of using violence to correct injustice or minimize harm is questionable even in cases that many regard as noncontroversial. Was the violence used by the Allies in World War II or by the North in the Civil War any more successful than alternative, less violent measures would have been? Who can say? There is at least some good reason in both cases to think otherwise.

Furthermore, and fifth, the decision to use violence to prevent future violence often has violent repercussions for innocent people, even in personal disputes. Put another way, though many people regard collateral damage as excusable, it is nonetheless violent, especially when it is both extensive and foreseeable. If I strike my wife, my children suffer collateral damage if they accidentally witness the incident. We know this. We know, too, that the decision to undertake war in modern times carries with it the unavoidable consequence that innocent third parties will be killed. As mentioned in the first chapter, rates of civilian deaths in modern war have increased dramatically over the past one hundred years. In World War II, for example, civilian deaths accounted for approximately half of all deaths or higher.[3] Data suggest that the figures for civilian deaths in most recent wars are approaching 90 percent![4]

Sixth, even the mere preparation to prevent violence can lead to violence. Between 1992 and 1995 the United States and its allies sold an astonishing amount of weaponry to other nations, this at a time when there was no credible threat by other nations to U.S. security. Today, not counting arms sales by former Soviet republics, the United States sells to other nations more weapons than are sold by all other nations combined. The United States sells approximately 73 percent of all weapons that third-world nations purchase. Even taking all nations into account, U.S. weapons sales or gifts account for approximately one-third of all such sales or gifts worldwide.[5] The United States does this in the mistaken belief that violence is sometimes necessary to prevent violence. But it was U.S. weapons that killed American troops in Somalia. The weapons that the UN was trying to wrest from rival factions in Somalia are part of the hundreds of millions of dollars worth of weapons "aid" that the United States gave to Somalia during the 1980s. In the previous decade the Soviet Union had supplied Somalia with weapons. Who trained the mujahideen who have now turned their rocket launchers on U.S. helicopters in Afghanistan? The CIA trained and funded them, in an effort to harm or weaken the Soviet Union, our erstwhile enemy. The United States also initially helped to develop Saddam Hussein's biological and chemical weapons.

Seventh, it is presumptuous to conclude that the only way to protect the innocent is by violent means. As Gandhi pointed out, people engage in conflict throughout their lives. Almost all conflicts are settled nonviolently. For millennia we have studied how to solve conflicts violently. It's only within the past century that we have begun to study just how conflicts are resolved nonviolently. If it's true that when the only tool one has is a hammer, then every problem looks like a nail, then it's also true that if we've only studied war and violence as means of putting an end to violence, then every problem will look as if it can only be resolved by violence. But those who study nonviolence have more tools than violence for protecting the innocent. Again, the latter chapters in this book will address just how.

Eighth, and finally, the argument that one must protect the innocent may well be one of the greatest contributing factors, if not the greatest contributing factor, to the deaths of innocents themselves. It can never be known for sure whether more people or fewer people would have died had Europe resisted Hitler as the Danes did, had Native Americans refrained from retributive attacks on the expansion of whites and attacks by whites in the West, had the Iraqi people resisted Saddam Hussein through nonviolent strategy. But it is not idle speculation. It's a question that deserves to be answered by trying nonviolence as a means of resisting injustice, as a means of defending the innocent. Organized violence has been tried for millennia. It has not put an end to attacks upon innocent people. Nonviolence has not been tried for long in an organized way. It may well be the case that more innocent people are better safeguarded by the use of nonviolence as a means of settling disputes than are safeguarded by violent means.

The United States is by no means the only nation that thinks it is safeguarding itself by providing weapons the world over. But the United States does so to a greater extent than any other nation. In 1967 Martin Luther King Jr. called the United States "the greatest purveyor of violence on earth today." The statement is still true. And it's hardly clear that such efforts succeed. Odd as it seems, many efforts—perhaps even most efforts—to reduce violence perpetrate violence, and in many instances such violence perpetrates even more violence than those efforts prevent.

One might dispute these responses to Archbishop Migliore's contention that sometimes violence is necessary, especially to protect the innocent, but this much is indisputable: every time two or more parties enter into a violent conflict, at least one of those parties loses. If a party knew in advance that they were going to end up the loser, that party would generally not enter the conflict in the first place. In short, no one can know that the violence that one employs will be successful in achieving one's aims. All that one can know is that if one employs violence to reduce violence, one is engaging in the very sort of behavior one is trying to prevent. In this important respect, preventive violence is decidedly *not* like a vaccine, which has a proven success rate with very little or infrequent collateral damage.

If we perpetrate violence, we can be assured that violence—the violence that we do—will occur. It *might* prevent some other violence. But often it will not. Furthermore, when we use violence, we increase the likelihood that violence will be used in response against us. Who will emerge victorious is almost always anyone's guess. More often than not the use of violence to prevent violence is a response to a crisis situation, a crisis that could have been averted had the situation been addressed earlier. But if we are serious about reducing violence, then we must rid ourselves of the myth that violence is sometimes necessary to prevent violence. We must substitute for that myth the trite but unpleasant truth that when we use violence, we do violence to others, often to innocent others. We must acknowledge that, like those who killed Jews in an effort to stop the plague, we often do not know the sources of the violence we are trying to overcome. We are often thrashing about in fear and confusion when we employ violence. We often do a good deal of harm with the best of intentions.

One cannot reach the end that one desires by pursuing means inimical to those ends. The reduction of violence cannot entail the use of violence. It cannot entail harming others intentionally or out of negligence. In Platonic terms, it requires that we not make others worse off. If one is making *any* others worse off, one is not engaged in reducing violence, at least not with any prescient assurance.

NOTES

1. Roger Fisher and William Ury, *Getting to Yes* (New York: Penguin Books, 1983).

2. Peter Ackerman and Jack DuVall, *A Force More Powerful* (New York: Palgrave, 2000), 207ff.

3. Matthew White, "Source List and Detailed Death Tolls for the Twentieth Century Hemoclysm," http://necrometrics.com/20c5m.htm (accessed October 10, 2012).

4. Ruth Leger Sivard, *World Military and Social Expenditures 1991* (Washington, D.C.: World Priorities, 1991), 20.

5. "TIV of Arms Exports from the Top 50 Largest Exporters, 2011–2011," taken from SIPRI Arms Transfers Database, Stockholm International Peace Research Institute, http://www.sipri.org/research/armaments/transfers/databases/armstransfers (accessed on Jan. 6, 2012).

Chapter Five

The Myth of Effective Punishment

Punishment is itself violence, and in the long run it is counterproductive as an effort to reduce violence. It is by nature violent, but most people believe it a reasonable practice nonetheless. Most people believe that those who do wrong deserve to be punished; that the more heinous the wrong, the more severe the punishment; that the more frequently someone perpetrates an offense, the more severe should be his or her punishment. These views are the prevailing myth.

Many justifications are provided for this myth. "Justice demands punishment," some say. "How else will people learn that what they did was wrong?" "We have to make an example of wrongdoers so that others will not be tempted." "Scum like him deserve to die." "Punishment deters others." These ideas are applied across the spectrum of human behavior, from scoldings or spankings in the home; to fines, imprisonments, or capital punishment at the national level; to sanctions, economic boycotts, and war at the international level.

Punishments all have in common the aim to deprive someone of a good—freedom, money, companionship, life itself—because that person or group has performed actions that are regarded as wrong. Usually the punishment is administered by some legitimate authority—a parent, a teacher, a state official, an army. The goods may be nothing more than some money, as in the case of a fine; they may be nothing more than time, as in the case of "time-out" for a child. Or they may be more substantial, as in the cases of imprisonment or execution or military attack. But for an action to be punishment, it must deprive someone of a good because of alleged wrongdoing on the part of that person or on the part of persons with whom that person is associated. [1]

Insofar as punishment aims to deprive someone of a good, for whatever reason or with whatever justification, punishment is thereby violent: it aims to harm someone. Justifications for punishment vary. Punishment is justified as a means of exacting vengeance—a means of satisfying in a relatively humane way the desire for revenge. However, even without vengeful motives, punishment can be viewed as a means of providing a wrongdoer with his or her just desert. People also seek to justify punishment as a means of deterring wrongdoers and potential wrongdoers from committing future wrongs. People seek to justify it by claiming that it can transform a wrongdoer, teach him or her not to do wrong. And to the extent that wrongdoers are obliged to perform services for the state or the victim, people also seek to justify it as a form of recompense or restitution. These various aims can be combined with one another, in varying degrees of emphasis. To be sure, there may be better ways of achieving any or all of these goals, but punishment, depriving someone of goods because of wrongdoing, nonetheless is often viewed as an effective, partial, or necessary way of achieving any or all of these purposes. Despite such claims, however, almost none of these justifications for punishment succeed. Let's see why, one at a time.

REVENGE

One reason why people seek the punishment of wrongdoers arises from simple outrage at having been wronged by another. When we are wronged, we grow angry, too. We want to vent our anger, and on whom better to spill out our anger than those responsible for our suffering? This is the notion of revenge. Revenge is part of what is heard in the cries of those who seek the death penalty for murderers. It is for the most part a strong or violent reaction to a sense of having been wronged, as in the case of a student of mine in the 1980s. She had volunteered in class to debate the issue of the death penalty, to which she was strongly opposed. I met with her at length on a Friday to review her presentation, which she was eager to deliver. On Monday she walked into class, apparently distraught. She asked if she could make her presentation right away and get it over with. I consented, and she took her place at a lectern. She said, "I have always been strongly opposed to the death penalty, but this past weekend my best friend was abducted and murdered in Florida. I hope they catch the bastards who did it and give them the electric chair. That's all I have to say." And then she ran out of the classroom.

This rather poignant example illustrates well the power of the call for revenge. When we feel wronged, we want to lash out. We want the person who has done wrong to suffer for his or her wrongdoing. We don't feel it's fair that the person should be happy, content, or continuing uninterruptedly his or her life. There's a strong inclination to make the person suffer in whatever way that person may have caused another to suffer. And the inclination is often an inclination to deliver the punishment ourselves and not to bother with an agent.

Revenge or retribution as a justification for punishment faces several problems, however. First, punishment may indeed satisfy a longing for revenge, but it succeeds in creating other victims: the friends and relatives of the wrongdoer, who may themselves be struggling to bring the wrongdoer back into harmony with his or her community. As such, revenge or retribution—even retribution without the emotional accompaniment of vengeance—thereby causes more pain, more injury, more violence, often to others who are utterly innocent. It creates a vicious cycle of violence.

Second, punishment rarely succeeds in satisfying the vengeful appetite. Most evidence suggests that retribution does not help a victim or a victim's friends and relatives overcome their loss to any greater extent than do other means. Sister Helen Prejean, in her book *Dead Man Walking*, speaks to this second concern with strong anecdotal evidence to which many of us can relate, at least to some extent. She quotes Vernon Harvey, whose daughter Faith had been murdered by Robert Lee Willie. Prior to Willie's execution, Harvey says that he can't wait to see the "smoke fly off his [Willie's] body." Later—but still prior to Willie's execution—Harvey spoke to his daughter's murderer and said that "he'd see his ass fry."[2] And how did Harvey feel after Willie's execution, which he witnessed? Six years after the murder, two years after the execution, Prejean reports, "He just can't get over Faith's death."[3] She says that his rage is not satisfied.[4] Harvey says to her later:

> Know what they should've done with Willie? They should've strapped him in that chair, counted to ten, and then at the count of nine taken him out of the chair and let him sit in his cell for a day or two and then

strapped him in the chair again. It was too easy for him. He went too quick. [5]

At another point he adds: "We're not executing enough of them." [6] It's clear that the execution of his daughter's murderer provided him no sense of relief.

An anecdote that reveals a different aspect of victims' relatives is related by Prejean earlier in her book. Prejean speaks of Lloyd Le-Blanc, whose son had been murdered. LeBlanc says that at the scene of the murder he had forgiven whoever it was who killed his son. He claimed that he did not attend the murderer's execution out of a spirit of revenge but rather in hopes of an apology from the murderer, an apology that he did, in fact, receive. However, even in this case, the apology did not assuage his occasional feelings of revenge either. [7]

One victim, the father of a woman killed by Timothy McVeigh in the Oklahoma City bombing of the Murrah Building, initially wanted to see McVeigh executed. But he changed his mind a few weeks after the bombing. He befriended McVeigh's father and sister, and he worked unsuccessfully to prevent McVeigh's execution. Since then he has spoken around the United States against the death penalty. His experiences echo Prejean's reports:

> I was speaking in Seattle recently. A lady told me she had always supported the death penalty. Her husband had been murdered in 1981, in Florida, and the murderer had killed other people, too. She had supported the death penalty right up until the execution of her husband's killer. Then, a week after the execution, she started to get this creepy feeling.
>
> This woman told me that when the murderer was alive, she could take her rage out on him. But once he was dead, she had nowhere to release the rage. The prosecutor never told her that she might go through this mental and emotional crisis once the guy was executed. She told me that if she knew then what she knows now, she would have done everything she could to stop that execution. I have heard that many times. So the death penalty can actually prevent healing, rather than helping. [8]

Another problem with carrying out revenge is that one often feels worse about oneself for having become a vengeful person. The student mentioned at the outset of this section no doubt thought of herself as loving and compassionate when she spoke with me on the Friday before her presentation. But by Monday morning she had become vengeful. Likely upon later reflection she would have a somewhat different image of herself than she had prior to her feelings following the abduction and killing of her best friend. People who perpetrate or desire revenge, at least when revenge is not institutionalized as part of one's culture,[9] often come to regret their own thoughts and actions.

Revenge is thus a justification for punishment, but the truth about revenge is that it is largely unsatisfying to those who seek it. It frequently fails to accomplish the desired purpose, and it inflicts violence on others, sometimes innocent others, and thereby perpetuates a cycle of violence.

RETRIBUTION

But perhaps the desired purpose of punishment is not merely satisfaction of the desire for revenge. Perhaps the desired purpose is retribution, giving someone what he has coming. This notion has been best captured, philosophically, by Immanuel Kant, who argued that wrongdoers should be treated in the same way that they treat others, that the rules by which they have chosen to live should be the rules by which they should be judged. Accordingly, murderers should be killed, thieves should have goods taken from them, and so forth. These actions should not be performed haphazardly but according to the rule of law, in an orderly and systematized manner. In this respect retribution avoids the dominant tone of revenge: it is simply a leveling of the balance of justice. And although rehabilitation can be a part of punishment, this particular model of punishment is not focused on rehabilitation: it seeks punishment, plain and simple, for the express purpose either of realigning the scales of justice or of demonstrating to the wrongdoer and others that justice has been done.

But problems persist even with respect to punishment as retribution. Most prominent among such problems is that sometimes no good will come of punishment. Or it may be that more harm will be done. Suppose the wrongdoer has a family who depends upon him or her. What then? Why should *they* suffer? Isn't *that* unjust? It is no use arguing that the wrongdoer should have thought of that: those who depend upon the wrongdoer may have had nothing whatsoever to do with the crime. Also important to our purposes here is that there is no reason to think that such punishment fulfills our sense of justice: victims don't necessarily get compensated for their losses under such a scheme. Indeed, they often continue to suffer. Furthermore, the wrongdoer may never come to appreciate his or her wrongdoing. The punishment is not designed to accomplish anything except an eye for an eye, or the value of an eye for an eye. But that value is not necessarily extracted in a way by which it can be redistributed to those who have been harmed. And even if it were extracted, as is often the case when the punishment is a fine, it frequently is not redistributed to the victims of the wrongdoing themselves. And unless that redistribution, that compensation, occurs, it is difficult to understand why a second loss balances the scales.

PUNISHMENT AS EDUCATION OR REHABILITATION

One might argue instead that by punishing wrongdoers, they are able to experience the wrongness of their actions, that the only way the lesson can be brought home is through punishment. Along similar lines, it is sometimes argued that those who do wrong benefit from being punished. Perhaps punishment of wrongdoers is good for them; perhaps if they are not shown in very powerful ways that society dislikes what they have done, then they will not learn to correct their own misbehaviors. With such ends in view, we assign penalties—fines or imprisonment—to those convicted of crimes. In some societies people are beaten, maimed, tortured, or publicly shamed. [10]

But wrongdoers are not likely to recognize that justice has been done because they usually lack a belief system similar to those administering the punishment. If I smoke marijuana, and all of my friends do, too, and none of us believes that we are any the worse for it, and I get sent to jail for twenty years for possessing marijuana, I'm not likely to believe that I did anything wrong. I'm likely to believe that the law is wrong, that society-at-large has a problem. In my mind the score is not evened at all; it is even more unbalanced.

Similarly, Timothy McVeigh murdered 168 people in a bomb blast in Oklahoma City on April 19, 1995. He was convicted of this crime and sentenced to death. Did the punishment teach him a lesson? Did he come to repent his wrongdoing? Six years after the bomb blast, awaiting execution in a jail cell,

McVeigh still maintain[ed that] he planted the bomb to "teach the government a lesson," in retaliation for federal raids at Ruby Ridge, Idaho, and the Branch Davidian compound in Waco, Texas. In an ex-

cerpt from letters sent to *The Buffalo News*, McVeigh called the bombing "a legit tactic."

Also on June 11, [2001,] *The Oklahoman Online* reported that
McVeigh had written letters to his hometown paper expressing regret
that he hadn't carried out a series of assassinations against police and
government officials instead. [11]

In short, punishment itself that aims at education or rehabilitation rarely
improves the attitudes toward society of those who are punished; more
often, it worsens those attitudes. To the extent that an individual or a
group in society regards the society-at-large as acting against their
interests, punishment is not likely to improve respect for the law; rather, punishment is likely to confirm the belief system of the offenders
that led them to break the law in the first place.

DETERRENCE

Many of us think that punishment deters. Not only do we believe that it
deters wrongdoers from engaging in further wrongdoing (sometimes
called *specific deterrence*), but we believe that it also serves as an
effective warning and reminder to others not to engage in wrongdoing
(sometimes called *general deterrence*). We attempt to justify our punishment of wrongdoers by appealing to these so-called deterrent effects: if we did not punish wrongdoers, the wrongdoers and others
would conclude either that there is nothing wrong with robbing, beating, raping, stealing, and so on, or that they, too, could perform such
horrible deeds and "get away with them." But by punishing wrongdoers, people who might otherwise do wrong are deterred from doing
so. Thus, the argument goes, punishment serves a useful purpose for
society at large. Not only does it deter wrongdoers from committing
further offenses; it also deters people who are not yet wrongdoers from
engaging in actions that are considered offenses.

As convincing as this line of reasoning may seem, the facts just
don't support it.

In the first place, it is not true that the more severe the penalty, the
greater the deterrent effect. In the United States, at least, states without
the death penalty have consistently had lower murder rates. In 1990, for
example, states without the death penalty averaged 0.04 fewer murders
annually per 100,000 population than states with the death penalty.
Since that time, the rates of difference have tended to be even greater.

In 2010, for example, the difference was 0.25, and the difference has been as great in a given year as 0.44 (1996 and 2003). [12] Further evidence of the death penalty's lack of deterrent effect crosses cultural borders, too: a study in the *British Journal of Criminology* reveals that the presence or absence of the death penalty over a period of fifty years had no effect on murder rates, which were relatively stable during years when execution rates varied and failed to drop when executions rose. [13]

Furthermore, U.S. sentences for noncapital crimes are generally longer than sentences for similar crimes in other Western democracies, and yet the United States has more people per capita in jail than any other Western democracy. Of course, part of the explanation for this could be that the United States has a higher per capita rate of incarceration simply *because* we keep people in jail longer than other nations. But at best that is only part of the explanation. One would expect that if severity of punishment deters, then nations that punish the most or the longest would have fewer criminals per capita. Such is most definitely not the case. "Research has failed to provide scientific proof that executions have a greater deterrent effect than life imprisonment and such proof is unlikely to be forthcoming." [14]

It is possible that the data above represent a simple correlation between murder rates and capital punishment, or that the argument above simply confuses cause with effect, or that a third factor would account for both the high incarceration rate and the high murder rate. But some evidence also indicates that murder rates *increase* in the weeks following an execution. [15] Such data suggest that violence begets violence, not that the penalties are not severe enough.

In the second place, in addition to data showing that more severe punishment for murder does not increase any deterrent effect that punishment might have, deterrence itself requires an efficient and effective criminal justice system. The number of murderers actually caught and sentenced in the United States, when compared to the number of murders committed, is approximately 50 percent. That percentage drops to 14 percent when speaking of assaults as opposed to murder. [16] That means that one has a one-in-two chance of getting away with murder and a seven-in-eight chance of getting away with assault. These statistics are hardly likely to deter. They suggest that deterrence might have more to do with getting caught than with getting punished.

Note that the fear of getting caught is not the same as the fear of getting punished. If one *knows* that one will be caught doing something wrong, then in most circumstances the action would be futile. It would only be useful if one wished to inflict some sort of irreparable harm on another, harm that could not be remediated. The killing of another human being is the prototypical example of irremediable harm, and it may explain why punishment of any sort for murder has little effect on those who would perpetrate it. Prior to the rise of gang violence in the United States during the 1980s, murder most frequently occurred between people who knew one another, suggesting that extreme emotions were at play in these events. People under such stress are not likely to be considering consequences of actions. Since the rise of gang violence in the United States, such murders account for approximately half of all murders. In such cases, neither "getting caught" nor being punished would likely deter. And in the other cases, the incentives to murder are apparently greater than the disincentives, if only in part because the odds of getting caught are slightly less than the odds of not getting caught. It follows, then, that punishment itself, at least for murder, is not a deterrent.

Of course, murder is not the only crime. Perhaps punishment works as a deterrent for other crimes? It doesn't, and the reason has a lot to do with the efficacy of any criminal justice system. Punishment or the threat of punishment is an extremely inefficient means of deterring people from wrongdoing. Is there any reason, for example, to believe that people have ceased selling or using marijuana because a government attaches criminal sanctions to its sale or use? Or that people who need to steal in order to survive will desist from stealing because a government attaches criminal penalties to the act of stealing? In order to prevent people from smoking marijuana or stealing, one must be able to convince them that if they attempt such actions, they will be caught almost every time they do it. Even if they are not punished, when people know they cannot succeed in doing something, they will not do it. We don't attempt to fly under our own "power" from tall skyscrapers. We don't attempt to take exams about whose subject matter we have no knowledge whatsoever. What would be the point? Punishment or the threat of it may deter some people some of the time, but generally it is ineffective unless it is almost certain.

Sometimes, too, punishment itself has the opposite effect of what is intended. Sometimes, that is, it encourages more wrongdoing. Punishment of sex offenders, for example, often leads to their committing more sex offenses, not fewer. The tightening of restrictions on released sex offenders, it is feared, could add to their stress. Jill Levenson, a professor at Lynn University in Florida, said that "'psychosocial stresses' have been linked to repeat offenses among criminals."[17]

RESTITUTION AND RECOMPENSE

Another reason why so many people believe that wrongdoers must be punished arises from the notion of fairness. Fairness seems to require that those who caused the suffering provide the recompense. If I am robbed or beaten, I suffer, and my suffering is caused by the person who robbed or beat me. If my nation is attacked by another nation, my nation suffers, and that suffering is caused by the nation that launched the attack. Since, all else being equal, there is no justification for my being robbed or beaten, or for my country being attacked, the misfortune is undeserved. And the party responsible for the misfortune should therefore make it up to the victim, should restore what was taken. This is the notion of restitution, or recompense, or restoration, that those who suffer unjustly at the hands of others ought to be able to recover those losses from the people responsible for the losses in the first place.

At a personal level, restitution can be as simple as a parent requiring her daughter to return to her brother a toy that she has taken from him, and perhaps to apologize as well and promise not to do it again. This view is especially evident in civil law and in recent victims' rights campaigns, through which people who have been injured by lawbreakers or by contract violations can seek reparations for the losses they incurred. At the international level, nations often seek reparations for war damages. The Treaty of Versailles, regarded by many as excessively punitive in the war reparations it demanded, is but one prominent example of this principle at work at an international level.

Technically speaking, however, restitution and recompense are not punishments. They are repayments. They are ways of "making up" for one's mistakes, but they are not punishments, as such, for one's mistakes. If someone has taken something unjustly, it is not a punishment to demand or expect that it be repaid. The wrongdoer is being deprived of goods, it is true, but insofar as the goods are repayments for what was unjustly acquired, they are not the wrongdoer's goods in the first place. This can be seen by looking at a simple example of wrongful harm such as a brother stealing his sister's toy. The parents may require the brother to return the toy, and they may also require the brother to give the sister one of his toys for the same period of time as he had been in possession of the sister's toy. This requirement is not a punishment; it is compensation, repayment. If the parents sent the brother to his room for "time-out," with or without requiring him to return the toy, *that* would be a punishment, and there would be nothing of recompense or restitution in such an action.

This can also be seen if one looks at the difference between civil law—also called the law of torts—and criminal law. Criminal law seeks punishment for people who wrongfully harm others. Civil law typically does not: when one person successfully sues another in civil court, the defendant would be expected to compensate the plaintiff for harm done, but only in special circumstances would the defendant also be punished with the assessment of a fine. Civil law rightly distinguishes between compensatory damages—damages that compensate someone for the harm they suffered—and punitive damages—damages that award something further, as a punishment to the wrongdoer. The distinction is itself proof that compensatory damages awarded a victim are not regarded as punishment, but, as the term suggests, as compensation or recompense.

It is thus a mistake to view restitution or recompense as forms of punishment. Strictly speaking, they are not. Wrongdoers in most instances can be required to repay or restore to victims and to society what they have taken. They can also be educated and rehabilitated, as is often done with alcohol-related driving offenders.

Sometimes, of course, a wrongdoer is a threat to others. Sometimes, as seems to be the case with some sex offenders, rehabilitation is not possible. What shall be done in such cases? Does concern about violent or ineffective treatments for offenders preclude us from locking them up? Clearly not. In such cases the offender is not being punished. The offender is simply being removed from society until the time—if any—that he or she can be returned to society as a nonthreatening member. The difference is one of attitude or tone. Locking someone up because one wants to "even the score" or seek retribution is the expression of a very different attitude than locking someone up because they cannot be trusted not to do harm to others again. Again, parents know this difference well. Often parents will send a child away from others until the child can assure everyone that he or she will "behave." The child is then allowed to return. Such an action is not a judgment of the intrinsic worth of the wrongdoer; it is a judgment of the extrinsic value of the wrongdoer's likely future actions. This is not punishment; rather, it is prudent regard for the well-being of others. It expresses concern for all.

CONCLUSION

Examination of the various justifications for punishment reveals each of them to be deficient. As a means of revenge, punishment fails to satisfy those who seek it. As a means of retribution, it rarely achieves justice for the victims, and it often creates new victims unjustly. As a means of deterring other wrongdoers, punishment doesn't work. And as a means of providing restitution to victims of wrongdoing, it is irrelevant: restitution can be provided without punishment, often more effectively and easily. Thus, none of the standard justifications for punishing wrongdoers appears to be easily supportable. Punishment is simply a violent act, an act that causes intentional or foreseeable harm and that serves no measurable purpose. It is time to discard the myth that wrongdoers should be punished.

Some may yet object that even if punishment fails to satisfy those who seek vengeance, even if punishment creates new victims, even if it doesn't deter, those who have done wrong still *deserve* to be punished, sometimes at whatever cost. Such a position is not easily dismissed; it is perhaps the most telling of the justifications for punishment. But one must acknowledge that even the worst of us have some redeeming qualities, that we ourselves sometimes do bad things, and that punishment is, regardless, a form of violence. After we acknowledge those truths, then it becomes a bit more difficult to insist that punishment is itself justified. At any rate, these questions will be addressed further in the final chapter.

NOTES

1. Sometimes people are not punished for their own actions but for the actions of those with whom they are associated by virtue of family, institution, country, and so on. This is a common tactic in schools and classrooms. As discussed earlier, it is called collective punishment and when applied by a nation against inhabitants of another country is a violation of international law.

2. Sister Helen Prejean, *Dead Man Walking* (New York: Vintage Books, 1994), 118.

3. Prejean, *Dead Man Walking*, 226.

4. Prejean, *Dead Man Walking*, 226.

5. Prejean, *Dead Man Walking*, 235.

6. Prejean, *Dead Man Walking*, 236.

7. Prejean. *Dead Man Walking*, 244–45.

8. Bud Welch, "Timothy McVeigh Killed My Daughter," Bruderhof Forgiveness Guide, http://www.forgivenessguide.org/articles/Bud-Welch.htm (accessed June 21, 2005).

9. Albanian and Afghan (Pathan) cultures are notorious for their embrace of revenge as a means of obtaining justice. It is doubtful that in such cultures people who perpetrate revenge come to doubt themselves or question the validity of their motives or their worth as people. See, for example, Majlinda Mortimer and Anca Toader, "Blood Feuds Blight Albanian Lives," BBC News, September 23, 2005, http://news.bbc.co.uk/2/hi/europe/4273020.stm (accessed June 28, 2012); and also Palwasha Kakar, "Tribal Law of Pashtunwali and Women's Legislative Authority," 4, http://www.law.harvard.edu/programs/ilsp/research/kakar.pdf (accessed June 28, 2012).

10. For example:

> "[In Malaysia] criminal law prescribes caning as an additional punishment to imprisonment for those convicted of some nonviolent crimes such as narcotics possession, criminal breach of trust, and alien smuggling. Judges routinely include caning in sentences of those convicted of such crimes as kidnapping, rape, and robbery. . . . Caning, which is carried out with a 1/2-inch-thick wooden cane, commonly causes welts, and sometimes causes scarring. The law exempted men over 50 and women from caning. Male children 10 years of age and older may be given up to 10 strokes of a light cane." *Country Reports of Human Rights Practices for 2007*, vol. 1 (Washington, D.C.: U.S. Department of State, August 2008), 878

This particular example does not make clear the aims of such punishment. This punishment above could be aimed at revenge, at instruction, or at deterrence. But it is at least reasonable to assume that among the aims of this punishment is that of instruction, of revealing to the offending party that what he or she did was wrong.

11. Ted Ottley, "Timothy McVeigh & Terry Nichols: Oklahoma Bombing," Crime Library, http://www.trutv.com/library/crime/serial_killers/notorious/mcveigh/updates.html (accessed on January 7, 2012).

12. "Deterrence: States Without the Death Penalty Have Had Consistently Lower Murder Rates," Death Penalty Information Center, http://www.deathpenaltyinfo.org/deterrence-states-without-death-penalty-have-had-consistently-lower-murder-rates (accessed July 2, 2012).

13. David F. Greenbert and Biko Agozino, "Executions, Imprisonment and Crime in Trinidad and Tobago," *British Journal of Criminology* 52, no. 1 (2012): 113 –40.

14. Roger Hood, *The Death Penalty: A World-wide Perspective*, rev. ed. (Oxford: Clarendon Press, 1996), 238, ¶328.

15. Prof. Ernie Thompson of the University of La Verne in California examined homicides in California after the reintroduction of the death penalty in that state. Thompson found increases in homicides during the months following the first execution. "Effects of an Execution on Homicides in California," *Homicide Studies* 3 (1999): 129 –50.

16. Bureau of Justice Statistics, U.S. Department of Justice, http://bjs.ojp.usdoj.gov/content/pub/html/cjusew96/cpo.cfm (accessed on January 7, 2012).

17. Michael Hill, "Experts Question Wisdom of Sex Offender Restrictions," *The Detroit News*, Associated Press report, June 21, 2005, http://www.detnews.com/2005/politics/0506/21/A04-222081.htm (accessed June 22, 2005).

II

Nonviolence

Chapter Six

An Overview of Nonviolence

Most of us would like to live in a world where we do not have to resort to the use of violence, but we are afraid that if we take the initial step in renouncing violence, we would become victims to those others who countenance or practice violence. Why, for example, should we worry about whether *our mere intentions* are violent if *others' actions* are already violent? Why should we give people who have already harmed us the benefit of the doubt and thereby open ourselves to letting them harm us again? Why should we put ourselves at a disadvantage, at greater risk, and reject the use of violence when others would use violence against us? Although many of us find it unfortunate to have to subscribe to the myths discussed in the preceding chapters, although we would like to discard them, we believe that we can only afford to adopt a new paradigm in a perfect world, and in the eyes of most people this world is not perfect. To commit to nonviolence in a less-than-perfect world is to impose upon oneself a handicap that most of us are unwilling to adopt. How are we to address successfully and nonviolently those who walk less gently in the world, the bin Ladens and Hitlers and, yes, even our own friends and relatives, and perhaps ourselves, whose behaviors sometimes anger us and elicit our worst sides? How, nonviolently, do we address injustice, do we address the threats of punishment or harm that confront us?

One important reason that most of us hesitate to adopt nonviolence is that we misunderstand it. We think that being nonviolent means giving up, giving in, and taking whatever our adversaries mete out to us. We think it involves largely ineffectual protests, civil disobedience, and going to jail. We think it would only work with "nice" governments or moral people. Two prominent scholars of nonviolent action, Erica Chenoweth and Maria Stephan, address this issue by highlighting two different approaches to nonviolence:

> Strategic nonviolent resistance can be distinguished from principled nonviolence, which is grounded in religious and ethically based injunctions against violence. Although many people who are committed to principled nonviolence have engaged in nonviolent resistance (e.g., Gandhi and Martin Luther King Jr.), the vast majority of participants in nonviolent struggles, have not been devoted to principled nonviolence. The conflation of nonviolent struggle with principled nonviolence, pacifism, passivity, weakness, or isolated street protests has contributed to misconceptions about this phenomenon. Although nonviolent resistors [*sic*] eschew the threat or use of violence, the "peaceful" designation often given to nonviolent movements belies the often highly disruptive nature of organized nonviolent resistance. Nonviolent resistance achieves demands against the will of the opponent by seizing control of the conflict through widespread noncooperation and defiance.[1]

Chenoweth and Stephan's characterization of nonviolence as two somewhat distinct camps helps to illustrate some misconceptions about nonviolence and some of the reasons for such misconceptions. But nonviolence, at least in practice, is more of a spectrum than it is two distinct camps, and this spectrum, too, helps account for misconceptions about nonviolence.[2] The spectrum reveals the variations in the degree and extent to which people renounce violence. So at the one extreme end of the spectrum is what one might call *selective nonviolence*, an approach that entails a rejection of violence in some of its forms for a limited time. This is a position that even the most violent of people hold, for even the most violent of people act nonviolently a good portion of the time. At the other end of the spectrum is what one might call *comprehensive nonviolence*, a renunciation of violence in its many forms and in every moment of one's life. Of course, people locate themselves on many different positions between these two poles, often moving along the spectrum as their own experiences, beliefs, or value systems change.

Many people whom we could classify as selective nonviolentists, for example, see nonviolent action as little more than one set of tools among many for attaining one's goals. Such people might also include those who practice what Gandhi called "nonviolence of the weak," nonviolence that is practiced because one has no other options and is afraid to risk much. Moving further along the spectrum from left to right (a direction not reflective of political orientations of left wing and right wing with respect to the various views on this spectrum) are those who recognize nonviolent action not just as an occasional tactic but as an entire strategy, comprising sets of tactics that are generally far more effective than are violent tactics in righting perceived wrongs, in overcoming oppression, and in wrenching power from those who abuse it. Typically, along this part of the spectrum, people are focused heavily on the renunciation of physical violence, and they pay less attention to renunciation of psychological or institutional violence. These are perhaps the people that Stephan and Chenoweth refer to as the "vast majority of participants in nonviolent struggles, [who] have not been devoted to principled nonviolence." Many but not all of these people employ nonviolence according to what Tom Hastings has called "the Kleenex principle": use it when you need it, and throw it away when you're done with it.[3] But somewhere across the middle of the spectrum one finds people who are either interested in renouncing a broader range of violent behaviors, including perhaps attitudes and thoughts, or in renouncing violence of all sorts on the basis of some ethical principle or personal preference, or both. Further toward the other end of the spectrum are people like Gandhi, Tolstoy, and Martin Luther King Jr., who attempt to integrate nonviolence into all aspects of their lives, on even a minute-by-minute basis. Accordingly we can speak of one end of the spectrum as *selective nonviolence* and the other end of the spectrum as *comprehensive nonviolence*.

It is interesting that while Chenoweth and Stephan reject the conflation of nonviolent strategic action with passivity and weakness, they themselves seem to suggest that a more comprehensive nonviolence is passive or weak. There need be nothing passive or weak about comprehensive nonviolence, just as there need be nothing passive or weak about many of the approaches to nonviolence that are less than comprehensive. Indeed, those who advocate nonviolent strategic action—without being comprehensive about their approach—are quite explicit about the strength of their approach. And although the center of concern for nonviolent strategic action is the social or political dimension—a desire to achieve social change—this is often a concern of comprehensive nonviolentists, too, some of whom might see passive action itself as a strong social practice.[4] However, the central concern of comprehensive nonviolence is the integration of the renunciation of nonviolence with one's daily practices, as an individual, as a member of a family, as part of a body politic. This plays out in various ways that will be examined later, but, briefly, it is often based on a belief that one must always respect persons, oneself and others, in all of one's actions. Sometimes this respect for the individual extends to individuals other than human beings, for example, animals, and it manifests itself in such practices and commitments as vegetarianism or sustainable living. Often, too, because of this respect for individuals, it entails a concern for social, political, or environmental justice and embraces as well many elements of more selective forms of nonviolence aimed at social and political change.

Selective nonviolence has been around for millennia, but only in the twentieth century, following the pioneering efforts and writings of Mohandas Gandhi, Richard Gregg, Joan Bondurant, and Gene Sharp, has it been studied as a technique that can be employed as a relatively clear set of tactics and strategies. Sharp has written a number of books on this subject, virtually all of them corollaries to his magnum opus, *The Politics of Nonviolent Action.*[5] A major subset of people who advocate nonviolent strategic action, including Gene Sharp, don't like the term *nonviolence*. They prefer to use terms such as *strategic nonviolent action*, *nonviolent struggle*, or *civil resistance*. Chief among such advocates are Peter Ackerman and Jack DuVall, authors of *A Force More Powerful: A Century of Nonviolent Conflict.*[6] Initially inclined to speak of strategic nonviolent action, more recently they have adopted the term *civil resistance*, and until very recently their focus was almost exclusively on the use of nonviolent action as a means of political change in countries outside of the United States.[7] Their nonprofit organization, the International Center on Nonviolent Conflict, has supported much research and training in the tactics and strategies that nonviolent action comprises. [8] Ackerman and DuVall follow the basic precepts of Sharp's pioneering work, and their influence has been dramatic. Through the promotion of Sharp's works, distribution of videos and DVDs that they have helped produce and fund, and workshops held around the world, they helped, directly and indirectly, to train the activists who overthrew the Serbian leader Slobodan Milosevic in 2000, the people who unseated Ukraine's Viktor Yanukovych in 2004–2005, and the leaders of the uprising that forced Egypt's Hosni Mubarak from power in February 2011.[9]

Comprehensive nonviolence, at least on the far end of the spectrum, understands nonviolence as a way of life, a way of behaving in the world. While it does not have social or political change as its focus, it may adopt strategic nonviolent action for social and political change under certain circumstances. More to the point, however, is that it takes the idea developed in the second chapter, that violence is the carrying out of an intention to do harm or of an intention to act in a way that is likely to cause harm, and applies this to a greater or lesser degree to one's entire life. Many people see Buddha, Jesus, Tolstoy, Schweitzer, and Gandhi as people who epitomized this way of life, a way of life that attempts to minimize harm to other life, that can embrace and encourage vegetarianism, meditation, and pacifism (not necessarily passivism), as well as strategic nonviolent action.

Gandhi and Buddha are people who carried this idea into all aspects of their lives. For them, a commitment to nonviolence was not only a commitment to minimize harm to other people but also a commitment to minimize harm to other animals and even plants. For many, such a commitment is difficult, even inconceivable. And so people who embrace comprehensive nonviolence understand their commitments in varying degrees, represented by different points along roughly half of the spectrum of nonviolence. Some attempt to practice nonviolence only toward people; others extend this to some forms of nonhuman animal life; still others extend this to plant life and to their own thought patterns.

Of course, the division between selective and comprehensive nonviolence is not neat, and that is why it is presented as a spectrum. Many people who adopt strategic nonviolent action as an alternative to war or violent confrontation find themselves drawn to comprehensive nonviolence; others do not. Some people who adopt comprehensive nonviolence reject some of the practices of strategic nonviolent action as forms of violence while many other such people find most or all of strategic nonviolent action to be a valid and potent political expression of comprehensive nonviolence. However, the entire spectrum of approaches makes clear that nonviolence, even in a less-than-perfect world, is preferable in at least one way or another—practically, strategically, morally, spiritually—to violence. In what follows we will explore in greater detail some of these variants of nonviolence, and we will see how, when practiced well, they are indeed preferable alternatives to our current mythology.

NOTES

1. Erica Chenoweth and Maria J. Stephan, *Why Civil Resistance Works: The Strategic Logic of Nonviolent Conflict* (New York: Columbia University Press, 2011), 10.
2. I am grateful to Duane M. Cady, whose book on pacifism—*From Warism to Pacifism: A Moral Continuum*, 2nd edition (Philadelphia: Temple University Press, 2010)—suggested to me the idea of understanding nonviolence, too, as a spectrum rather than a smattering of specific and distinct positions.
3. Tom Hastings, Portland State University. Private conversation in San Francisco, October 16, 2004.
4. Many strategic nonviolentists who tend toward the comprehensive side of the spectrum see noncooperation with authorities, a refusal that is passive, as quite powerful and effective. Rosa Parks, the woman whose refusal to leave her seat on a bus in Montgomery, Alabama, in 1955 launched the famous Montgomery Bus Boycott, might be an example of such a person.
5. Gene Sharp, *The Politics of Nonviolent Action* (Boston: Porter Sargent, 1973). Other books by Sharp include *Gandhi as a Political Strategist* (Boston: Porter Sargent, 1979) and *Waging Nonviolent Struggle: 20th Century Practice and 21st Century Potential* (Boston: Extending Horizons Books, 2005).
6. Peter Ackerman and Jack DuVall, *A Force More Powerful* (New York: St. Martin's Press, 2000). *A Force More Powerful* also served as the basis for a two-part PBS television documentary by the same name.
7. Now Ackerman has turned toward attempting to influence U.S. electoral politics as well. See Thomas Friedman, "Make Way for the Radical Center," in *The New York Times Sunday Review*, July 23, 2011, http://www.nytimes.com/2011/07/24/opinion/sunday/24friedman.html?_r=1.
8. http://www.nonviolent-conflict.org. Scholars and activists from around the world have benefited from the support of the center and generated other books on the subject such as Kurt Schock's *Unarmed Insurrections: People Power Movements in Nondemocracies* (Minneapolis: University of Minnesota Press, 2005) and *Why Civil Resistance Works: The Strategic Logic of Nonviolent Conflict* by Erica Chenoweth and Maria J. Stephan (New York: Columbia University Press, 2011).
9. Sheryl Gay Stolberg, "Shy U.S. Intellectual Created Playbook Used in a Revolution," *The New York Times,* February 16, 2011, http://www.nytimes.com/2011/02/17/world/middleeast/17sharp.html?pagewanted=all.

Chapter Seven

Selective Nonviolence

Everybody uses nonviolence. We just don't think of ourselves as using it. When we are in conflict with others, we often talk things out calmly. We negotiate. We write letters, go back and forth between friends trying to ascertain truth to resolve misunderstandings. All of these are nonviolent behaviors. Even the most violent people among us are by and large nonviolent. In these respects all of us practice selective nonviolence.

Perhaps a rule—in Kant's terms, a maxim—is at work subconsciously or sometimes consciously when we engage in such behaviors. It is probably not a rule that says, "Avoid violent behavior at all costs." More likely it is a rule that says, "Avoid violent behavior when you can because it is usually more destructive than other alternatives." If we twist this rule around a little bit, we might formulate a more precise rule, something like this: "I should generally act nonviolently because nonviolent actions properly conceived and executed are in the long and short terms generally less destructive than violent actions." This is the sort of rule that underpins, consciously or unconsciously, selective nonviolence.

The first decade of the twenty-first century saw a major upsurge in the use of selective nonviolence on the socio-political level, due in large measure, first, to the work and teachings of Gandhi and the 1982 film that bore his name; second, to the scholarship of Gene Sharp and the proliferation of his books and teachings; and third, to the efforts of

Peter Ackerman and Jack DuVall through their organization, the International Center on Nonviolent Conflict.

Gandhi is an ambiguous figure to many. Was he a religious man with a political bent or a political man with a religious bent? It is difficult to read Gandhi's writings and conclude from them anything other than that he was primarily a religious man who pursued God, or Truth, as he preferred to called God, through individual, social, and political practice. Nonetheless, Gene Sharp, a Gandhi scholar, interprets him as a political strategist. In Sharp's early years he himself was inclined toward what he saw as Gandhi's comprehensive or principled nonviolence, but over time Sharp altered his own views. By the time Sharp completed his book *The Politics of Nonviolent Action*, he had become convinced that nonviolent action need not be linked to ethical or moral principles and that indeed it may actually be more effective or likely to be adopted if it is not linked to ethical or moral principles. *The Politics of Nonviolent Action* and his other works since that time strongly reflect that orientation.

Selective nonviolence often uses powerful strategies for achieving social and political change, and Sharp's works are masterful in explaining how. Indeed, it is fair to say that virtually no one writing since the 1973 publication of *The Politics of Nonviolent Action* has said anything about strategic nonviolent action that would contradict or refute Sharp in any serious way. So an understanding of selective nonviolence and its efficacy is best understood, at least initially, by understanding Sharp's theory of power and strategy.

SHARP'S THEORY OF POWER

At the outset of his three-volume work, Sharp distinguishes between two views of power; he calls them the monolithic model and the pluralist-dependency model.[1] These are not two kinds of power. Rather, they are two ways of looking at the same set of circumstances. Sharp utilizes a pyramid or pillar structure to explain.

At the top of the pyramid, or supported by the pillars, are the rulers, whose rule is enforced by those at the next level below, the enforcers. Enforcers include police, army, judges, district attorneys, and so on. And the largest group, the base of the pyramid on which the entire structure rests, is the rest of the people, neither rulers nor enforcers.

Sharp says that one can understand this structure in either of two ways, either as a monolithic power structure or a pluralist-dependency power structure. In the monolithic model, rulers and enforcers are seen as those who possess the power and exercise it over the masses of people. In the pluralist-dependency model, rulers and enforcers are seen as possessing power only to the extent that the masses below are willing to accept or at least tolerate it. Sharp argues that the pluralist-dependency model is a more accurate reflection of reality, for without the support of the masses, without their consent or obedience,[2] the top of the pyramid would enjoy no support and would fall.

Power, Sharp contends, arises from a variety of sources: material resources such as money, capital, means of production; human resources such as numbers of people, education of people, skill levels of people; the ability to inflict punishment on others; charisma associated with leaders; natural resources; means of transportation; and so on. Often leaders and enforcers control these sources of power, but their ability to maintain their control over these sources depends upon another source of power, the extent to which people are willing to obey the leaders and enforcers. Sharp spends a few pages on the psychology of why people obey, emphasizing such reasons as habit, fear of sanctions, moral obligation, self-interest, identification with the leader, zones of indifference, and absence of self-confidence.[3] We can understand all of these reasons by breaking them into three categories. Doing

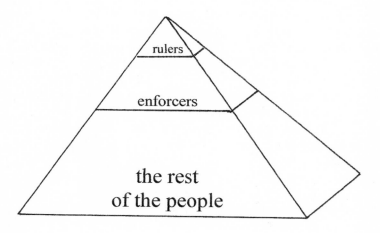

Figure 7.1.

so will help us to understand better the dynamics of nonviolent strategy when we come to it shortly.

People obey their leaders and the rules of the countries or organizations to which they belong for at least one of three reasons, and it makes no difference whether we are talking about the leaders or rulers of a country, a corporation, a school, or a club. The same sorts of reasons underpin people's obedience regardless of the size of the organization or institution. First, people may obey their leaders or conform their behaviors because they have internalized the values of their leaders. Second, they may obey because they identify with the country, the organization, or the leaders. Third, they may obey simply because they fear what will happen to them if they do not. Let's examine these one at a time.[4]

When people have *internalized* the values of their leaders, or when they believe that their leaders exemplify the values that the membership or population hold dear, leaders need do very little to get people to conform their behaviors to a norm. For example, my values have been formed over decades now, and one value that I cherish is the right to speak freely and to allow others to speak freely. Leaders of my institution or of my government do not need to encourage me or prompt me to defend that value; I do it all by myself. No enforcement is necessary.

When people *identify* with a figure or a group—the minister in their church, the CEO of their corporation, the leader of their government, their peers, the fellow members of a society—that identification will carry them a long way toward behaving in ways that match the behavior or at least the expectations of that leader. For instance, when I was young, I identified strongly with the Beatles and with another rock 'n' roll group: Crosby, Stills, and Nash. I still wear my hair and dress as they did. Nobody makes me do it. I do it of my own free will. Similarly, many youths today are fond of piercings and tattoos. It's the way they identify with each other. Nobody makes them get tattoos and piercings. They do it because they *want* to.

But when people have *not* internalized the values of the leadership of their country or institution, or when they do *not* identify with leaders, the leaders must rely upon force and upon enforcement to get people to conform their behaviors to some norm or other. For instance, few people like to obey posted speed limits on roads and highways. People tend to drive a few miles over the speed limit . . . unless they see a police car in their mirror or along the side of the road. Then they conform their behaviors to the expected norm. When the police car is out of sight, the foot goes down again on the gas pedal.

Now, one could get everyone to obey the speed limit by posting police cars and police officers every few hundred yards along every road. But it would be a very expensive proposition. Far better if people identified with the police or with the reasons for the posted speed limits. Even better if people internalized the values that led to such postings. Again, for example, when I drive through a small village, I almost always obey the speed limit because it seems to me that the danger of hitting a small child if I am speeding in a small village is a lot greater than the danger of my hitting a small child if I am speeding 70 miles per hour instead of 65 miles per hour on a freeway. I identify with the people who live in that town and respect their posted speed limits. No police officer is necessary to get me to obey speed limits when I drive in a village, but a police officer is necessary to get me to obey speed limits on an expressway, especially if there is little traffic along a long, open stretch of road.

Of course, as Sharp points out, the rulers and enforcers can use fear to keep the masses in line, and to the extent that they are successful in generating and maintaining fear, they can remain in power. But it is the job of nonviolent activists to help the masses overcome fear if the masses are interested in change. This change may be little more than a desire to see a policy or rule altered, or it may be as dramatic as the overthrow of a dictator or an entire government. This sort of account of power explains very neatly the falls from power of Slobodan Milosevic in Serbia and Hosni Mubarak in Egypt, as we shall see.

It is costly in terms of money, human effort, and capital, however, for rulers and enforcers to maintain their power through the use of fear, and this partly explains why nonviolent action is often more effective than violent action. If the leaders of a country or institution are legitimate authorities, enjoy the respect of the people, are duly constituted, and so forth, then it is rarely necessary to employ force to exact obedience and consent of the people they govern. This is because the leader represents the values that the people themselves hold, whether we are talking about a country, a corporation, a school, or a club. The people in such instances do not fear their leaders: they identify with him or her or them. This is the strongest sort of bond between rulers and the people they govern. The amount of force necessary to govern is minimal.

But sometimes the leaders of a group or a nation do not enjoy the support of the people. Sometimes they don't represent the values of the people, or sometimes the people simply don't identify with their leaders or those entrusted with enforcement. Under these circumstances the leaders and enforcers must rely upon enforcement, upon force, to exact conformity. And here is where Sharp's theory and nonviolent strategy in general become particularly relevant.

When compliance is forced upon people, the people must fear the consequences of not complying. If they don't fear those consequences, then the leaders and enforcers lose their power. So leaders whose people neither identify with them nor respect them must rely on tough enforcement. But if the people become emboldened, then even tough enforcement may not matter. Tough enforcement, which relies, ultimately, on violence, on the ability to harm those who disobey, has, in the words of Jim Lawson, "a fairly simple dynamic: I hurt you until you cry 'uncle.'"[5] Expressed another way, the dynamic is: "Do as I wish, or I will make you suffer." But nonviolent strategy, according to Sharp, helps people overcome their fear of what the rulers and enforcers can do to them, and when this happens, power begins to shift.

THEORIES OF NONVIOLENT STRATEGY

In 1963, in his "Letter from Birmingham Jail," Martin Luther King Jr. identified four basic steps for any nonviolent strategy or campaign.[6] They were:

1. collection of the facts to determine whether injustices exist
2. negotiation
3. self-purification
4. direct action

The King Center later modified these steps as follows:[7]

1. information gathering
2. education
3. personal commitment
4. negotiation
5. direct action
6. reconciliation

The information gathering in step one is about the same as King's earlier step of collecting the facts. Education entails a reaching out to the wider community to inform people of the grievance. Personal commitment is similar to the idea of self-purification, entailing an honest assessment of the degree to which one is willing to sacrifice for the cause. Negotiation is an ongoing process, something to which a grievance group should always be open. Direct action involves the kinds of activities that most people usually associate with nonviolent action: sit-ins, strikes, boycotts, but also less severe actions such as leafleting, lobbying, and so on. Reconciliation is a final step when the grievance has been addressed satisfactorily. Ideally it involves extending a hand of friendship to those against whom one has struggled in an attempt to heal any wounds that the nonviolent action might have opened up.

Gene Sharp has articulated a process similar to King's, but it is much more fully developed, and, although he places little or no emphasis on reconciliation as a final step, the strategic approach outlined by the King Center and the strategic approach developed by Sharp have many similarities. So first we will look at Sharp's theory of strategic nonviolent action. Then we will examine the differences between his theory and other approaches to nonviolent strategy.

To begin with, in every conflict, one finds two parties—or more—at odds with each other. However, often one also finds others who have little stake in the outcome of the conflict, or at least who believe they have very little stake in the outcome of the conflict. Nonviolent strategy engages those third parties in ways that violent conflict cannot. How?

In violent conflicts, all parties to the conflict are engaged in causing harm to the other parties in very obvious ways. Sympathies of parties more or less external to the conflict are not roused so easily. The outsiders see the vicious behavior on the part of all the parties in the conflict. But if one party to the conflict steadfastly refuses to engage the other side violently, then the violent treatment of that side by the opposing side elicits sympathy and wonder from those who would normally stand on the sidelines. The uninvolved parties wonder why the nonviolent party to the conflict is being treated so badly when it is clear that they do not wish to bring physical harm to anyone. The more one side suffers, nonviolently, at the hands of the other, violent side, the less likely is the violent side to win more and more advocates to their cause. This can and often does lead to an increase of power—in Sharp's sense of the term—to those engaged in nonviolence and a decrease in power to those engaged in violence: people withdraw their tacit support for the violent side, and with that withdrawal of support is a sapping of their material and nonmaterial resources. Even those engaged in enforcing policies violently may come to have second thoughts about what they are doing and may lose their balance.

Gene Sharp calls this effect *political jiu-jitsu.* He describes it as a loss of balance felt by those who use violence against nonviolent adversaries. The effect has been observed in many nonviolent struggles, and it is a crucial pivot point for strategic nonviolent action. Nonviolent strategy relies on generating this loss of balance among one's opponents. A familiar example, Gandhi's Salt March, will help to illustrate this effect.

In 1930 Gandhi decided to march from his ashram on the Sabarmati River near Ahmedabad south 240 miles to the ocean beach at Dandi, just south of Bombay, what is now called Mumbai. The march took about three weeks, and along the route many people joined him so that by the time he reached Dandi, thousands of Indians were present to watch him publicly violate the salt laws that gave Britain a monopoly on salt production in India. For fear of sparking larger protests, Britain did not dare arrest Gandhi at this time. However, so many Indians began making salt as Gandhi had done that the British authorities soon began arresting those who did. Eventually, the authorities arrested Gandhi, too, and by this time some tens of thousands of Indians had been jailed for making salt. The government, though stronger in one sense, began to look foolish for jailing Indians for making salt and came under intense pressure by its own citizens in Britain to relent. The backlash against the authorities for such a violent response to this nonviolent protest caused a loss of balance for the British Empire, eventually leading them to release everyone from jail and to invite Gandhi to England to discuss the possibility of Indian independence from Britain. Although in the short term the Salt March failed to win any major concessions from the British, it alerted the world to the colonial exploitation of India by the British by eliciting much sympathy for the Indian cause, and in the long term it probably helped convince Britain to reduce and release its colonial hold on India.

Gandhi's Salt March illustrates the jiu-jitsu effect of using violence against nonviolent resisters. It also highlights many other aspects of the strategy that Sharp recommends. For instance, the march began on a small scale and grew gradually over time. This had the effect of slowly creating pressure on the British government. It also had the effect of slowly overcoming fear among those who opposed it. Gandhi's timing was also deliberate: he began the march shortly after the Indian National Congress issued a declaration of independence and timed the march to arrive at the sea approximately on the anniversary of the Jallianwala Bagh massacre, an attack by the British in a garden in the city of Amritsar in 1919 that left hundreds of defenseless Indians dead. The march also began with innocuous activity: a walk. It ended with an act of civil disobedience, and it continued a month later with an attempt to wrest control, nonviolently, of British production of salt at the Dharasana Salt Works, about twenty-five miles farther south of Dandi.

Timing, symbolic actions, gradual increases in pressure, slowly but steadily overcoming fear—all of these are some of the many aspects of the strategy that Gene Sharp put forward in *The Politics of Nonviolent Action*. The strategy ideally comprises a variety of nonviolent tactics, discussed in detail in volume 2 of the same work.

In that volume Sharp divides the various tactics that nonviolent strategy comprises into three broad categories: protest, noncooperation, and nonviolent intervention. When he wrote *The Politics of Nonviolent Action* in 1973, he identified 198 tactics of protest, noncooperation, and nonviolent intervention. With the advent of personal computers, cell phones, and the Internet, one could easily conceive of fifty to one hundred more tactics that would also fit into his categories. Sharp arranged these tactics in a roughly ascending order of risk and commitment.

Generally an oppressed population loses its fear by engaging first in protests of one kind or another. Protests range from simple letters to the editor to lobbying delegations to petitions, from symbolic acts to musical performances to walkouts at meetings, all of which are activities that typically involve far less risk than tactics further down the list. When an individual realizes through her protests that she is not alone, that thousands or tens or hundreds of thousands stand with her, she begins to shake off her sense of fear, begins to feel more powerful, and, if necessary, can more easily engage in more forceful tactics such as noncooperation.

For example, whenever I have started a grassroots political organization, I have usually begun by having a social event with food: a barbecue, a pizza party, some wine and cheese—some food that draws people to the event. I don't disguise the purpose of the event: to talk over some issue of concern to a variety of people. But the entertainment aspect of the event helps the event appear successful even if little about the issues of concern is accomplished at first. It also allows people to see that there are others with similar concerns. This is empowering, and it helps to reduce fear. From such an initial gathering, further meetings arise, strategies and tactics are formed, subgroups are established, and the group has begun.

Many people inexperienced in nonviolence—and even people experienced in nonviolence—believe that one has to engage immediately the powers-that-be in some form of protest or civil disobedience, but Sharp's first forty or fifty actions suggest almost nothing of the sort. Mostly the tactics involve raising concerns about an issue, publicizing it, trying to persuade people to change their minds. The tactics involve informing others about the issue in question, meeting or writing those in a position to address the issue, publicizing one's cause, organizing lobbying groups, writing letters to the editor, producing pamphlets, and so on.[8] To this list one could now add such tactics as establishing listserves and websites, producing YouTube videos and Facebook pages. *The Collected Works of Mahatma Gandhi*[9] contain page after page, letter after letter, of his writings directed to people or institutions with which he had grievances. It is actually rather boring to read through them except that they illustrate how much nonviolent persuasive effort he put forth into his causes ceaselessly and repetitively long, long before he undertook action in the form of demonstrations, fasts, civil disobedience, and the like.

Often, one can achieve one's objectives without ever resorting to noncooperation or intervention. Often wise leaders change their minds quickly upon seeing how many people are aggrieved about some policy or other. Often it is enough for them to see the potential for a loss of their power and the rise of some alternative leader. Moreover, it is crucial that a group with a grievance not commit themselves to risks and tactics that people in the group are not committed to carrying out. So it is wise to spend a good amount of time and effort in building one's group, educating them in the issues, preparing them for what further tactics may be necessary, all the while increasing the size and commitment of the group.

After identifying fifty-four tactics of protest and persuasion, Sharp continues his list with more than one hundred more tactics of noncooperation, which he divides into three types: social, economic, and political noncooperation. Social noncooperation involves such activities as boycotting organizations at odds with one's stance or shunning people who maintain ties with such organizations. Economic noncooperation includes such actions as boycotts, but the noncooperation can develop into strikes—initially such symbolic actions as one-minute strikes (which can be lengthened bit by bit as a means of developing solidarity and applying greater pressure), but later industry-wide or general strikes. Political noncooperation begins with individual actions such as refusing to cooperate with institutional or government officials and refusing to obey rules or laws. On a larger scale, they can involve such action as removal of diplomats from another country, severance of diplomatic ties, or ousting organizations or countries from international organizations.

The most extreme types of nonviolent tactics are what Sharp terms interventions, of which Sharp lists forty. They include the sorts of actions that most people associate with nonviolent action: sit-ins, take-overs of institutions, and, ultimately, the establishment of alternative institutions that displace the institutions whose policies or leaders are oppressive.

If these tactics are put together creatively, likelihood of success in achieving one's political or social goals is excellent. First a grievance group must educate itself about its concerns. Then it should inaugurate a period of public education about the concerns, creating an awareness that an issue exists. As this is done, the group should begin to identify further tactics that might need to be employed down the line. Ideally, tactics are combined: if a color or a song or a symbol—or all three—have come to represent an issue to the wider population, then that color or song or symbol becomes part of every other tactic. One might begin a march with everyone wearing a T-shirt and singing a song, and the march might begin at one symbolic place and end at another. I recall, for example, one demonstration in Rochester, New York, in the early 1980s that began at the Federal Building and ended at the Liberty Pole. The 1963 civil rights March on Washington culminated, quite appropriately, at the Lincoln Memorial.

A grievance group should always be open to negotiation. In fact, it might be entirely appropriate to say that the goal of a grievance group is to achieve negotiation, at least as a starting point for change. If, early on, one can negotiate an end to the problems that generated concern, there is no need to bring forward nonviolent tactics that require greater commitment. But a group should be prepared to bring forward tactics requiring greater commitment if necessary. To that end the group must grow and identify which of its members are prepared to make what kinds of commitments to the cause. The group must also maintain nonviolent discipline, for if the group resorts to tactics that seem violent to third parties, the group will not grow in strength, nor will it likely diminish the power of its opponent. The Rochester, New York, march in the early 1980s, mentioned above, was somewhat unsuccessful insofar as hecklers distracted a few marchers and enticed them into a shouting match. It was the shouting match and not the concerns of the marchers on which the television news focused later that evening.

Fear of loss of power will eventually bring an opponent to a negotiating table. So a group must be well versed in negotiating tactics, as well. However, in the final analysis a group must remain disciplined in *nonviolent* action to attain the kind of power that will bring about meaningful change. However, here is where Sharp's theory of nonviolent action begins to part ways with the strategies of Gandhi and King.

NOTES

1. He also discusses these views of power and many of his other views summarized here in his more recent volume *Waging Nonviolent Struggle* (Boston: Extending Horizons Books, 2005).

2. Psychologists will often speak of conformity when talking about why people follow a leader. Sociologists and political scientists will tend to speak of obedience when discussing why people follow a leader. While the two concepts are not the same, for our purposes we can simply regard them as different sides of the same coin, one focused on group behavior, the other on individual behavior within a group.

3. Gene Sharp, *The Politics of Nonviolent Action* (Boston: Porter Sargent Publishers, 1973), 19–24.

4. The distinctions between these three reasons for obedience are taken from guest lectures delivered in my classrooms in the late 1980s by a professor of social psychology at St. Bonaventure University, Carl Wagner.

5. James Lawson, "Nashville," *A Force More Powerful*, PBS, September 2000, http://www.aforcemorepowerful.org/films/afmp/index.php (accessed on January 7, 2012).

6. Martin Luther King Jr., "Letter from Birmingham Jail," in *Nonviolence in Theory and Practice*, 3rd edition, edited by Robert L. Holmes and Barry L. Gan (Long Grove, Ill.: Waveland Press, 2012), 104–16.

7. The King Center, "Six Steps of Nonviolent Social Change," http://www.thekingcenter.org/king-philosophy#sub3 (accessed October 10, 2012).

8. Sharp, *The Politics of Nonviolent Action*, 117–82.

9. Mahatma Gandhi, *The Collected Works of Mahatma Gandhi*, http://www.gandhiserve.org/cwmg/cwmg.html (accessed January 7, 2012).

Chapter Eight

Toward a Theory of Comprehensive Nonviolence

Interestingly, the works of Gene Sharp and those who have followed him in writing about nonviolent strategic action are notably devoid of any detailed or extended discussion about what constitutes violence and nonviolence, let alone any sustained discussion about the moral value of nonviolence versus violence. Sharp's writings and the writings of those who follow him tend to see nonviolent action as nonviolent simply insofar as it eschews physical violence against persons. Thus, in Sharp's catalog of 198 nonviolent actions in volume 2 of his *The Politics of Nonviolent Action*, one can find such actions as "taunting one's opponents," "rude gestures," "destruction of one's own property," "fasts of moral pressure," and so on. These actions and others in the list are arguably violent, at least from the perspective of people like Gandhi who stand closer to comprehensive nonviolence on the spectrum of nonviolence than does Sharp. But insofar as they eschew physical violence toward other people, Sharp and many other selective nonviolentists regard such actions as nonviolent.

THE IMPLICATIONS OF A FULLER ACCOUNT OF VIOLENCE

One criterion for determining whether or not such actions are violent is the definition offered at the outset of this book: one does violence if and only if one acts with the intent to harm or with the intent to perform an action whose consequence is reasonably foreseeable as likely to cause harm. Harm in this context was to be understood as physical, psychological, or institutional. On this account, many of the tactics undertaken by so-called nonviolent activists are, in fact, violent. But even if one rules out this wider understanding of violence as a criterion and adopts the more common view of violence as physical harm to people, it becomes clear that many of the tactics identified by Gene Sharp and utilized by others are far less likely to strengthen the nonviolent strategy than are tactics that avoid psychological and institutional violence. The following example helps to illustrate this.

I was in college in the late 1960s, and during this time at my university, the University of Rochester, many students were demanding that the university divest itself of stock holdings related to the defense industry. This was an effort on the part of some of us to put pressure on the war industry in hopes of ending the Vietnam War. The president of the university at this time was W. Allen Wallis, adviser to Presidents Eisenhower and Nixon. He was perceived among many of the students as the university's personification of the powers directing the war effort. So some people did not like him, some did, and others did not concern themselves with him one way or the other.

From time to time, when the weather was warm, he could be seen walking across the main quadrangle of the campus when many students were sitting about on the lawn of the quadrangle. It was not uncommon for him to be greeted with a low volume of hissing, a kind of booing as he strode across the quad. I remember that, at the time, *even though I opposed the war in Vietnam and was not sympathetic toward W. Allen Wallis and the university's holdings in the defense industry*, the hissing that greeted the university president disturbed me. It alienated me from those with whom I normally felt in solidarity, and it made me think of the university president a bit sympathetically. In short, the taunting of this man had a jiu-jitsu effect, but *in the wrong direction*! Yet taunting is one of the allegedly nonviolent actions that Sharp lists in his catalog of nonviolent tactics. So, too, is the haunting of public officials, as well as rude gestures, as mentioned earlier.

These tactics aim to belittle or demean the individuals at whom they are directed, and because of this such tactics could be regarded as a form of psychological violence. This is why the jiu-jitsu effect works in the wrong direction in such instances. It inclines those people who are indifferent to a particular struggle to become sympathetic to the object of the taunts, not to those who perpetrate the taunts. And on another level, it is also why it is important, when considering nonviolent strategy, to have a thorough understanding of the nature of violence and not to limit oneself to thinking solely or primarily in terms of physical violence. W. Allen Wallis only looked better as a result of these tactics, which, in reality, are not nonviolent tactics at all.

SELF-SUFFERING AND COGNITIVE DISSONANCE

Sharp most likely got the term *jiu-jitsu* from Richard Gregg, who studied Gandhi's nonviolent techniques in the 1930s and described this effect in his book *The Power of Nonviolence*.[1] It's interesting that Gregg called this effect *moral jiu-jitsu* but Sharp prefers the term *political jiu-jitsu*. Sharp argues explicitly that his term is broader in scope, encompassing the loss of balance felt by those who use violence against nonviolent adversaries. But Barbara Deming, a nonviolent activist of the second half of the twentieth century, also speaks of this loss of balance as *vertigo*, following Frantz Fanon's use of the term in his book *The Wretched of the Earth*.[2] The vertigo of which she speaks has a decidedly moral flavor to it, arising from the disorientation one feels after resorting to violence against fellow human beings. Even Fanon, who advocates violence, speaks of this condition as a moral reaction to one's own use of violence. In light of such observations, it is apparent that moral reactions to tactics are in some way relevant to nonviolent strategic action. It is important to understand such relevance.

James Lawson described the dynamic of violent action as: "Do as I wish, or I will hurt you until you cry 'uncle.'" But the dynamic of nonviolent strategic action is, in capsule form: "Do as I wish, or make me suffer." Although many contemporary advocates of strategic nonviolent resistance would reject this self-suffering aspect of the dynamic of nonviolent action, the rationale for such a dynamic can be found in Gandhi's philosophy. Gandhi believed that nothing finite—no stone, no cow, no human being—can comprehend Truth, can comprehend all that is. Thus, as was mentioned earlier, for Gandhi, to destroy something that exists is to destroy a little bit of Truth, to preclude oneself from coming closer to ultimate reality, for Gandhi equated God and Truth. So, for Gandhi, at least, nonviolence is a means to Truth, a means to God. Thus, one must stand for what one believes is true, but since each one of us is finite, one must not do violence to another being, for in doing so one reduces the possibility of attaining Truth.

Put less abstractly, there is always more than one story to a conflict. To destroy one such story in a conflict, to prevent one side from presenting their views or from having their day in court, is to do violence to Truth. Conflicts are not solved by one side prevailing over another; they are solved by all sides coming to a workable understanding. Thus, pragmatically speaking, one should not do harm to other parties to a conflict because such harm interferes with coming to a workable understanding; the dynamic of violence—Do as I wish or I will hurt you until you cry "uncle"—is far less effective than the dynamic of nonviolence—Do as I wish or make me suffer.

There is another advantage to the nonviolent dynamic: often one party does violence to another because that party fears the other. A group that refuses to do violence *of any sort under any conditions* to another party goes a long way toward reducing the fear that the one party has of the other. And if the fear can be overcome, or at least diminished, then meaningful communication and understanding can, perhaps, begin. But meaningful communication and understanding cannot take place when both sides are doing all they can to harm each other.

We've already seen how Gandhi's Salt March placed the British in an awkward position. Either they had to do as Gandhi wanted and allow him and others to make salt, or they had to cause Gandhi and others to suffer. Gandhi set up the situation in this way. He put the British in a position of having to react to him, but he did no harm to them. The choice was theirs, and therein lay the nonviolence to his strategy. A few other examples may help make this strategy even clearer.

My university, steeped in the Catholic tradition, has long had rules that prohibit the presence of men in women's dormitories and women in men's dormitories beyond certain hours of the night. At a time when most universities were eliminating such rules, my university was still strictly enforcing them. One of my students suggested a strategy to challenge these rules. She suggested that women invite a priest into their dormitory to conduct a mass for men and women after the curfew hours. University officials would then be forced either to abandon the rules or prohibit the mass; they would be forced to decide which was more important to them.

Similarly, during the lead-up to the 2003 invasion of Iraq, my peace group wanted to distribute antiwar leaflets to attendees at a well-attended basketball game at my university. We knew we would be stopped from doing so because it would be politicizing an event and annoying fans. So we decided to print up the Pope's statement condemning the planned war and distribute that. Again, the university would have to decide whether they wanted to allow an antiwar message or censor the Pope, forcing them to decide which value was more important.

THE IMPORTANCE OF OFFERING A CHOICE TO ONE'S ADVERSARIES

In each of the examples above—the example of the dormitory rules, the example of the antiwar leaflets, and the Salt March—the nonviolent activists offered a choice to their adversaries: allow us to do as we wish or cause us to suffer. In each of the instances above, what the activists desired to achieve was something relatively small: holding a mass, leafleting some people at a sporting event, making salt. But the alternatives—fining people and stopping a mass, arresting people for trespassing and censoring the Pope, or stopping individuals from making salt and jailing them—were far more harsh in the eyes of most people standing on the sidelines. And the choice about which to allow was up to the authorities, the adversaries of the nonviolent activists. So in the end, either the nonviolent activists get their way, or the authorities and others perceive the response as an extreme measure to put a halt to behaviors that, on the face of it, are relatively innocuous, though their long-term ramifications are more serious.[3]

This aspect of nonviolent strategy is not only a matter of putting a choice to the opponent: "Do as I wish, or make me suffer." It is also what psychologists would call an effort to create cognitive dissonance. Cognitive dissonance causes people to experience surprise, shame, embarrassment, confusion, or humiliation when they discover that two or more of their beliefs are at odds with each other. Cognitive dissonance often forces people to choose between their beliefs, and one goal of nonviolent strategic activists should be to create cognitive dissonance in adversaries and in those uncommitted people who "sit on the fence" in a conflict, supporting neither one side nor the other.

So nonviolent strategic activists, ideally, should create a sense of shame, surprise, humiliation, confusion, or embarrassment in those who initially oppose their goals or in those who are initially indifferent to them. But they cannot *aim* to do so, for this would be a form of psychological violence. They can only do this by giving their adversaries a realistic and legitimate choice. Otherwise, they will fail in provoking shame or embarrassment. Here's why.

Shame and embarrassment, for example, each entail a belief in the people experiencing either of these emotions that they are somehow responsible for the actions that caused them shame or embarrassment. People experiencing shame believe that they or someone with whom they are closely connected have done something wrong. People experiencing embarrassment believe that others perceive them as having done something wrong. But if nonviolent activists are perceived as inciting behavior designed to cause shame or embarrassment, then they, the nonviolent activists themselves, will be perceived as the party responsible for the behavior. They, and not those in whom they aim to create shame or embarrassment, will be blamed. And then there is nothing about which to feel shame or embarrassment.

For instance, if a group of street demonstrators aim to provoke an army into becoming violent in order to create the jiu-jitsu effect, but they provoke the army with taunts and insults, the provocation will be seen by those standing on the sidelines as a provocation, a deliberate provocation, and the army will not be faulted for its response unless the response is overwhelmingly brutal. But if the street demonstrators offer the army a choice, say, "Side with us or arrest us for congregating peacefully in Tahrir Square," and then the army arrests them or beats them, the protesters will have likely succeeded in creating the desired jiu-jitsu effect. Their aim would not have been to provoke the army. Their aim was to give the army a choice. Their well-designed, creative nonviolence helps to create the cognitive dissonance among undecided parties and perhaps even among some in the opposition.

This unfortunate circumstance—that many who advocate so-called nonviolent resistance do not fully appreciate its dynamic—is even more manifest when one considers that Sharp and those who follow his lead allow for four possible outcomes of nonviolent strategic action. They are: reconciliation, accommodation (of at least some of the grievance group's demands), coercion, and disintegration of the opponent's institutions.[4] Certainly reconciliation can be considered an appropriate end for nonviolent action. Accommodation, too, where an adversary, grudgingly or not, bows to demands of a grievance group, is compatible with nonviolent action. But coercion and disintegration may well be ends incompatible with nonviolent strategic action, depending upon what one means by *coercion* and the manner in which disintegration of a power structure occurs.

Three recent examples of nonviolent strategic action at differing levels will help to illustrate these points a bit more fully. The election that deposed Slobodan Milosevic as president of Serbia in 2000 utilized many nonviolent tactics in a grand strategy that, at least on one or two levels, was successful. The Arab Spring also used many nonviolent tactics to overthrow or attempt to overthrow leaders of several Arab countries. In Egypt, street protests and public pressure led to President Hosni Mubarak's sudden resignation and departure from office. But the lack of a grand strategy was responsible in part for the lack of success in achieving what many of the people involved in the demonstrations desired. More importantly, failure to maintain nonviolence led to more widespread killing in Egypt than in Serbia during the popular uprisings, even though both regimes were brutal. And an even more extreme case of failure to maintain nonviolence is that of Syria, whose resistance abandoned nonviolence relatively quickly and turned to violence, the long-term outcome of which, like that of Egypt, still remains to be seen.

AN EXAMPLE: SERBIA

The Serbian revolution of 2000 was not exactly a revolution: it became a demand that election results be honored. Slobodan Milosevic, who had held power in the Federal Republic of Yugoslavia since 1990, was about to be forced from the presidency by term limitations. However, the Yugoslav Parliament changed the rules for selection of a new president, making it a possibility for Milosevic to be elected by popular vote for another term. Because the opposition was divided into so many parties, it was expected that Milosevic would win that election. In fact, when opposition parties united, he lost, but he refused to acknowledge his loss, attempting to fake the election results. In the end the people prevailed over him.[5]

How this all came about was the result of the work of many different groups, but especially a group of students and former students who had united earlier under the name of Otpor! (Serbian for *resistance*). A widely distributed film, *Bringing Down a Dictator*, documents how Otpor! reorganized and began to help galvanize much of the population of Serbia in opposition to Milosevic. They gained their inspiration from Gandhi and Martin Luther King Jr., and in the process of developing strategies, many of which were humorous or satirical in nature, they also discovered the work of Gene Sharp, whose ideas paralleled and augmented their own. Remaining largely decentralized to avoid being destroyed by arrests of leaders, keeping humor at their core, and urging the opposition parties all to unite behind a single candidate, they succeeded in helping to build a strong anti-Milosevic coalition. [6]

Perhaps the single biggest accomplishment of Otpor! was their success in helping the Serbian population overcome their fear of Milosevic. Probably even before they were introduced to the works of Gene Sharp, they had recognized the value of using humor and satire in their critique of the Milosevic government. Their ability to laugh while criticizing made it difficult for the government to rise above them, and it also made it possible for the population to laugh with them and, through laughter, lose their fear and become more serious of purpose as their strength and numbers grew. The film *Bringing Down a Dictator* illustrates a few of their humorous tactics: one clip in the film shows Otpor! members encouraging people on the street to view an eclipse through a telescope. When the people look in the telescope, they see the face of Milosevic being eclipsed. Another clip shows a few young students making fun of the Milosevic government's claim that the group is a terrorist group, highlighting how dangerous they are because they read a lot and wear glasses. Prior to Milosevic's forced departure, the BBC reported:

> Activities have included displaying an effigy of Mr Milosevic which passers-by could punch after paying one dinar; or painting red footsteps on the pavement—what they claimed to be Mr Milosevic's bloodied steps—leaving office for the final time.
>
> Otpor's symbol of a clenched fist has been displayed in a wide variety of places—from posters to T-shirts.
>
> Although some of these activities may appear frivolous, Otpor's campaign has done much to dispel fear among those who want to show their opposition to the government.
>
> And for long periods of time, while the rest of the opposition was in a state of slumber, Otpor demonstrated that there was a group of people who were prepared to overcome an all-pervasive apathy and demonstrate against the regime. [7]

In the end, Otpor! was instrumental in helping to unite various factions opposed to Milosevic, and their insistence on nonviolent tactics ensured that when Milosevic refused to give up his office, the successful demand that he step down was achieved with virtually no physical harm to anyone.

In the years since Milosevic was forced from office, various administrations have held sway in Serbian politics. One of the leaders of the efforts to hold Milosevic to the genuine outcome of the elections that turned him out of office, Zoran Đinđić, eventually became prime minister of Serbia, but shortly thereafter he was killed by an assassin connected with organized crime and the secret police in Serbia. Ten years after Milosevic was forced from office, Tomislav Nikolic was elected to the office of president in Serbia. Nikolic was formerly a compatriot of Milosevic, and some Serbs doubt that he has changed his stripes. However, unlike Milosevic, he has been a willing participant in a democratic process of elections in Serbia. So despite the ups and downs in Serbia of administrations that hark back to the days of Milosevic and assassinations in addition to that of Zoran Đinđić, Serbia has established itself as a relatively stable democracy that owes much by way of thanks to the nonviolence that turned Milosevic out of office. However, the experiences of Egypt and Syria in the decade after Serbia's "revolution" provide stark contrast in varying degrees to Serbia's experience.

SOME OTHER EXAMPLES: EGYPT AND SYRIA

In 2011 President Hosni Mubarak had ruled Egypt for thirty years. Although initially his rule helped to stabilize Egypt's economy, eventually he became perceived by his own people, Muslims, Christians, and secular Arabs alike, as a corrupt dictator. In early 2011, following Tunisia's successful overthrow of its leader, demonstrators throughout Egypt began protesting Mubarak's rule, demanding that he step down.

The demonstrations were widely perceived as spontaneous, but in some respects they had been years in the making. A *Foreign Policy* article documents how "in the summer of 2009, Mohamed Adel, a 20-year-old blogger and April 6 activist, went to Belgrade, Serbia." Adel had been the leader of a group called the April 6 Youth Movement, which had organized an unsuccessful 2008 textile mill strike in Egypt. Adel wanted to learn from the Otpor! activists, who had founded a training organization called CANVAS (Center for Applied NonViolent Action and Strategies), how to organize more successfully. "In Belgrade, Adel took a week-long course in the strategies of nonviolent

revolution."[8] One likely result of Adel's training is that, according to
the *Foreign Policy* article:

> The protests were a model of unity, tolerance, and nonviolent discipline.
> The different groups put aside their individual flags and symbols to
> show only the Egyptian flag and to speak, as much as possible, with one
> voice. Protesters swept the square clean and protected shops, detaining
> looters and making them give back the stolen goods. Coptic Christians
> in Tahrir Square formed ranks to protect the Muslims while they
> prayed; when the Christians celebrated Mass, the Muslims formed a
> ring around them. Together they embraced soldiers and faced the police
> with roses. They sang songs and wore silly hats. It had an authenticity
> that was uniquely Egyptian, but it was also textbook CANVAS.[9]

Indeed it was textbook CANVAS. When I first saw footage of the
demonstrations in Tahrir Square, I recognized immediately the symbol
of the clenched fist, the use of whistles, and the conviction that if
enough people converged for a long enough period of time and demanded the ouster of their leader, it would happen.

But there were important differences. One important difference is
that Serbia was accustomed to elections, and the election in which
Milosevic was ousted was the result of years of organizing on the part
of various political parties. Mubarak's ouster was not the result of an
election, and in the weeks that led up to his resignation, many citizens
were killed in the demonstrations calling for his removal. In the months
that followed his fall, Egypt lacked the relative stability of Serbia, and
the long-term outcome of the Egyptian "revolution" was very much in
doubt. A July 9, 2012, *Time Magazine* cover story about Egypt was
titled "The Revolution that Wasn't: Why The Generals Remain Egypt's
Real Rulers," and even though the generals had been stripped of some
of their power six months after that article, the newly elected president
of Egypt was widely perceived as beginning to assume dictatorial powers.

One of those who led the Otpor! movement is a well-spoken and
charismatic man named Srdja Popovic. Popovic was a cofounder of
CANVAS in the years after Otpor!'s success. He and others in CAN-
VAS helped to train people in other countries who were interested in
ousting those in power. These countries included Ukraine, Georgia,
Lebanon, Tunisia, the Maldives, Egypt, Burma, Zimbabwe, Iran, and
Venezuela.[10] Popovic has an excellent theoretical understanding of
how nonviolence works, both tactically and strategically, and he has

practical experience as well. He explains the relative success of the Serbian people in establishing a democracy in a way that highlights Egypt's difficulties. Says Popovic:

[In order to have] real democratization revolution itself is not enough. You need to follow up with capacity building and strengthening the democratic institution to get to a democratic society. Serbia was lucky to get it, and sometimes I think that some other countries like Georgia were really missing part of this "post traumatic" support from both their leading nonviolent movements and world democracies. [11]

Popovic might just as easily have said "Egypt" instead of Georgia.

The civil war that began in Syria in March 2011 as a series of nonviolent protests provides an even greater contrast to the example of Serbia. Not much groundwork had been laid in Syria for a nonviolent uprising against the government, and people had little to no practice in the exercise of representative government and democracy there. So after nonviolent demonstrations in various cities throughout Syria were met with violence at the hands of the Assad government, understanding of strategy and appropriate responses to violence was minimal, and nonviolent discipline, if any existed in the first place, was easily broken.

When Popovic last spoke with activists from war-torn Syria, he tried to persuade them that a boycott of state companies, not armed conflict, is the most effective tactic.

"Something similar worked perfectly in the Republic of South Africa a decade ago," Popovic said. "A number of state enterprises depend on domestic demand, and it is their money the government still uses."

Recent research supports Popovic's approach. In the 2011 study *Why Civil Resistance Works* [cited in chapter 6, earlier], U.S scholars analyzed more than 300 attempts at civil resistance over the past 100 years and found that nonviolent movements were more than twice as effective as their violent counterparts at achieving stated goals. "As soon as protests turn into an armed conflict, it is a kind of defeat," Popovic said. "It's like challenging [Mike] Tyson to a boxing match. Why not play chess with him instead? Our playing field is called creativity." [12]

While Popovic understands strategic nonviolent action well, perhaps as well as anyone, it is clear that he regards strategic nonviolent action as a means to an end and not an end in itself. Strategic nonviolent action, or civil resistance, is still aimed at overcoming an opposition, still aimed at winning. Strategic nonviolent action, then, by any other name, is still a battle. Unless it is coupled with a commitment to nonviolence as a way of life, it still sees the world in terms of "good guys and bad guys." While its ideal practice may recognize psychological and institutional forms of violence in addition to physical forms of violence, while it may ideally aim at conversion of opponents, ultimately, without being coupled to nonviolence as a way of life, it is in the final analysis a war by other means.

TOWARD COMPREHENSIVE NONVIOLENCE

That strategic nonviolent action—at least as presently conceived—is war by other means becomes more evident when one contrasts Gene Sharp's earlier writings with his later writings and compares them both to Gandhi's thought. Chenoweth and Stephan's distinction between strategic nonviolent action and principled nonviolent action (noted earlier in chapter 6) echoes a passage from Sharp's *Politics of Nonviolent Action*:

> Nonviolent action has often been practiced, and in a vast majority of the cases led, by nonpacifists who saw it only as an effective means of action. The popular idea that only pacifists can effectively practice nonviolent action—a view sometimes pressed with considerable conceit by pacifists themselves—is simply not true. [13]

Thomas Weber notes this position of Sharp and claims that it is a very different position from the views he held earlier as an emerging scholar:

> Speaking of the Palestinian Intifada, Sharp makes the points that "it is not a question, is this violent or nonviolent. It is not a question, is this morally right or morally wrong. It is not a question, is it justified or unjustified. Those are the ways it is usually argued among Palestinians. The question is, what are its consequences?" In Gandhi's philosophy the consequences of actions cannot be known in advance, and that is precisely why the means, over which there is control, must be kept pure. Sharp has moved a long way from the position he had adopted in his earliest Gandhian writings. [14]

Sharp—and Ackerman follows him on this point—believes it best to pursue strategic nonviolent action because it is effective, not because it is nonviolent. If it were not effective in achieving political goals, Ackerman—and perhaps Sharp—would be less enthusiastic about it. But Sharp is subtle in his claims about what constitutes strategic nonviolent action. While he is at pains to deny that nonviolent action requires a religious or moral commitment, he does think that effective nonviolent action requires a commitment to nonviolence that is close to, if not identical with, a moral commitment. He contrasts what Gandhi called the "nonviolence of the weak" and the "nonviolence of the strong." In his book *Gandhi as a Political Strategist*, he quotes Gandhi on the "nonviolence of the weak": "But their nonviolence, I must confess, was born of their helplessness. Therefore it was the weapon of the weak. [W]hat we practiced during the last thirty years was not nonviolent resistance by passive resistance which only the weak offer because they are unable, not unwilling, to offer armed resistance."[15]

Sharp characterizes the "nonviolence of the strong," on the other hand, as: (1) adherence to nonviolence even in crises; (2) application in all areas of life; (3) resourcefulness; (4) creativity; (5) use of the intellect; and (6) bravery in the face of severe repression.[16] Sharp is anxious that nonviolence of the strong not be "equated with belief in nonviolence as an ethical or religious principle."[17] Yet he neglects to mention in this summary that Gandhi also believed that nonviolence of the strong was a creed despite his having quoted Gandhi on this matter a page earlier: "Nonviolence of the strong cannot be a mere policy. It must be a creed, or a passion, if 'creed' be objected to."[18] In the final chapter of *Gandhi as a Political Strategist*, Sharp corrects himself on this matter, stating explicitly that nonviolence of the strong entailed as a primary characteristic an adoption of nonviolence as a creed. Still, Sharp insists that a creed of nonviolence means nothing more than "(a) that it would not be given up in favor of violence in difficult times and (b) that nonviolence would be applied in all areas of life." He is extremely reluctant to allow that nonviolence of the strong entail a religious, ethical, or principled commitment to nonviolence.[19]

It is difficult to see the difference between what Sharp means by a creed and what he means by a principled commitment to nonviolence. In the end, it seems, Sharp is a bit more willing than some of his protégés and followers to recognize that strategic nonviolent action tends to be more efficacious if it is linked to an unwillingness to resort to violence and if nonviolence is applied to all areas of life. The desirability of such a creed sounds more comprehensive than selective, though Sharp's protégés and followers may not be willing to grant the

necessity, let alone the advisability, of adopting nonviolence as a principle or creed.

This strategic nonviolent action, this civil resistance, this "war by
other means" has distinct advantages over standard warfare. For one,
fewer people are killed. For another, as Chenoweth and Stephan's studies point out, it has a higher success rate than standard warfare or
revolution. Yet another advantage is that it leaves open a much greater
possibility for reconciliation and harmony than does standard warfare.
Ultimately, however, it doesn't change the culture, even if it is nonviolent or less violent than other means.

Evidence that it doesn't change the culture, that it is a "war by other
means," can be found in the fact that various organizations with close
ties to the U.S. government have been involved in funding at least some
of these nonviolent uprisings in other countries. Freedom House, the
National Democratic Institute, and the International Republican Institute were all involved in helping to fund Otpor! and student organizations in Ukraine, Georgia, and Egypt. While these organizations are
officially NGOs (nongovernmental organizations), the people at their
helms include numerous U.S. senators and congresspeople such as John
McCain and Tom Daschle and former U.S. military leaders and State
Department officials such as Brent Scowcroft, Donald Rumsfeld, Ken-
neth Adelman, and Madeleine Albright. Furthermore, even though the
uprisings in these countries did represent the genuine will of a substantial proportion of their populations, it's also fair to say that these NGOs
were more than happy to contribute funding to support these people's
aims because they also furthered the aims of their own country, the
United States. One can only wonder what the reaction would be if the
United States were to discover that the Green Party was being funded
by such organizations in Russia or China, or if the United States were
to discover that the Tea Party were being funded by Neo-Nazi groups
in Europe, or if China were to discover that demonstrations in Beijing
were being funded by Freedom House, the National Democratic Institute, or the International Republican Institute.

Many selective nonviolentists or theorists like Sharp or Ackerman
are focused on success in achieving political goals that may or may not
involve conversion of opponents. Regardless, self-suffering, while perhaps not critical to other kinds of "success," such as coercion or grudg-
ing accommodation or disintegration of an existing power structure, is
extremely helpful in converting those who sit on the fence, those initially indifferent to the conflict, to shift their allegiances and thus shift

the balance of power. In this way self-suffering can also contribute to these other kinds of "success." It is also crucial to reducing the fear in one's opponents that one is out to destroy them or hurt them. Thus, selective nonviolence has many strategic and tactical advantages over warfare and other forms of physical conflict. But it remains at its best a strategy, a set of tactics, for achieving victory over others, and as such it differs only in means, not in ends, from other forms of conflict and warfare. Granted these means are valuable, insofar as they save lives and reduce harm, but they do not get at the heart of violence.

NOTES

1. Richard B. Gregg, *The Power of Nonviolence*, 2nd rev. ed. (New York: Schoken, 1966), 44–45.

2. See Barbara Deming, *Revolution and Equilibrium* (New York: Grossman Publishers, 1971); and Frantz Fanon, *The Wretched of the Earth* (New York: Grove Press, 2005).

3. Barry L. Gan, "Loving One's Enemies," in *Nonviolence in Theory and Practice*, 3rd edition, edited by Robert L. Holmes and Barry L. Gan (Long Grove, Ill.: Waveland Press, 2012), 306–13.

4. Sharp, *Waging Nonviolent Struggle: 20th Century Practice and 21st Century Potential* (Boston: Extending Horizons Books, 2005) , chapter 33.

5. "Milosevic: No Signs of Bowing Out," *BBC News*, July 6, 2000, http://news.bbc.co.uk/2/hi/europe/822194.stm (accessed on November 11, 2012).

6. *Bringing Down a Dictator*. Written, produced, and directed by Steve York. (Washington, D.C.: York Zimmerman, Inc.), 2001.

7. "Analysis: Otpor's Challenge to Milosevic," *BBC News*, May 15, 2000, http://news.bbc.co.uk/2/hi/europe/749469.stm (accessed November 13, 2012).

8. Tina Rosenberg, "Revolution U," *Foreign Policy*, February 16, 2011, http://www.foreignpolicy.com/articles/2011/02/16/revolution_u?page=0,0 (accessed on December 3, 2012).

9. Rosenberg, "Revolution U."

10. Bryan Farrell and Eric Stoner, "Bringing Down Serbia's Dictator, 10 Years Later: A Conversation with Srdja Popovic," in *Waging Nonviolence*, October 5, 2010, http://wagingnonviolence.org/author/bryananderic/ (accessed on November 13, 2012). See also Ivica Petrovic, "Serbian Non-violence Group Shares Know-how with Egyptian Activists," *Deutsche Welle*, March 28, 2012, http://www.dw.de/dw/article/0,,14846311,00.html (accessed November 10, 2012); and David D. Kirkpatrick and David E. Sanger, "A Tunisian-Egyptian Link That Shook Arab History," *The New York Times*, February 13, 2011, http://www.nytimes.com/2011/02/14/world/middleeast/14egypt-tunisia-protests.html?pagewanted=all&_r=0 (accessed on November 13, 2012).

11. Farrell and Stoner, "Bringing Down Serbia's Dictator."

12. Tomas Sacher, "The Exporters of Revolution," *Next in Line*, October 10, 2012, http://nextinline.eu/the-exporters-of-revolution/ (accessed on December 3, 2012).

13. Sharp, *Politics of Nonviolent Action* (Boston: Porter Sargent Publishers, 1973), 68.

14. Thomas Weber, "Nonviolence Is Who? Gene Sharp and Gandhi," *Peace & Change* 28, no. 2 (April 2003): 256, quoting from Sharp's *Gandhi as a Political Strategist* (Boston: Porter Sargent, 1979).

15. Sharp, *Gandhi as a Political Strategist*, 99.

16. Sharp, *Gandhi as a Political Strategist*, 106.

17. Sharp, *Gandhi as a Political Strategist*, 105.

18. Sharp, *Gandhi as a Political Strategist*, 105.

19. Sharp, *Gandhi as a Political Strategist*, 298–99. Much of the text in this and the preceding paragraph comes from the following book review: Barry L. Gan, untitled review of Gene Sharp, *Gandhi as a Political Strategist*, *The Acorn: Journal of the Gandhi-King Society* 5, no. 2 (1991): 27–29.

Chapter Nine

Comprehensive Nonviolence

> The means may be likened to a seed, the end to a tree; and there is just the same inviolable connection between the means and the end as there is between the seed and the tree. —M. K. Gandhi, *Hind Swaraj*, chapter 16

The "inviolable connection between the means and the end" to which Gandhi refers above weighs heavily against the five myths discussed in the preceding chapters. A violent act is violent, we have seen, not because of the end it achieves—or fails to achieve—but because of the intention one had in carrying it out. First, the intention to do harm—or to act in a manner that any reasonable person could see would cause harm—infects whatever means one chooses toward one's end: a beneficial or fortuitous end to an event can still be the result of someone's doing violence. Second, a person's being "bad" is often intimately bound up with his being "good": many of the worst atrocities in the world had been intended to bring about good, but the means used were harmful. Third, one cannot do violence with the expectation that one will put an end to violence. In using it, one perpetuates it. Fourth, punishment, unless its intention is to educate, to rehabilitate, to restore community, is itself a violent means. And fifth, nonviolent strategic action, insofar as it is strategic, is ultimately about winning, not ultimately about acting in ways not to cause harm. Although nonviolent strategic action works more often than violence, nonviolence seen as a means inextricably bound up with its end always works when one's aim is to *be nonviolent*.

Comprehensive nonviolence accepts fully Gandhi's point in the epigraph above: means and ends are inseparable. If one desires a nonviolent outcome, then one must practice nonviolent means to achieve that outcome. Thus, in principle though not in practice, selective and comprehensive nonviolence represent different outlooks on violence. For comprehensive nonviolence, nonviolence must be both means and ends.

In his signature work *I and Thou*, Martin Buber identified two ways—the only two ways, as far as he was concerned—of living in the world, of interacting with anything and everything.[1] One way of interacting with something in the world is to speak in the voice of *I-It*; the other way is to speak in the voice of *I-Thou*. The voice of *I-It* is the voice of the daily and mundane; it is also the voice of means and ends and of strategy. The voice of *I-Thou* is the voice of the holy, the voice of the divine, the voice of the sacred and profound; it is the voice of the eternal present. Understanding these two voices can shed some light on comprehensive nonviolence even though Martin Buber was not himself speaking explicitly of violence and nonviolence.

The voice of *I-It* is the voice of utility: one relates to something because of the value it offers one. I use a fork; I eat some food; I drive a car; I am friendly with someone because they have a toy I like, a piece of property I like, or a position from which they can help me advance my career. There's nothing wrong with many *I-It* relationships. Without them, human beings could not survive. But in certain circumstances they can be disrespectful, insulting, even violent and harmful to one or both of the parties. I might use a knife or a computer regularly because it has utility for the work that I do. But if I *only* use it and do not treat it with care, respecting it for what it is, it may cease being a functioning knife or a functioning computer. And then it loses its functional value, and I lose a tool that I need. I might value a friend because of what the friend has to offer me, but if I value that friend and others *only* for what I can gain from the friendships, I may in the end lose my friends, lose their respect, or become myself the sort of person I might despise.

An *I-Thou* relationship, on the other hand, exists entirely in the present. It does not see the *Thou* for what it was or for what it may be. It is just with it, not *in time*, but *out of time*, in the eternal present. It may *have* functional value, but that functional value is not the determinant of the relationship. I love my daughter and my son regardless of what they do; I take care of my cats, not because they bring me enjoyment but because I am with them. The love is unconditional; it is not experienced as a means to an end. Buber would say that it is not even experienced; it just is.

Comprehensive nonviolence, at its best and strongest, speaks in the voice of *I-Thou*. The means become the ends because there is no end other than *being* nonviolent. Similar to Kant's notion of moral duty, the nonviolence that one practices is practiced because it is nonviolence one wishes to obtain; it is not practiced for any other reason. This is not to say that this is a fully realizable and permanent circumstance for any human being. But it is an ideal by which we can fashion ourselves and our actions and, in so doing, address far more successfully the scourge of violence.

HOW COMPREHENSIVE NONVIOLENCE ADDRESSES THE FIVE MYTHS

Those who lean toward comprehensive nonviolence recognize the many ways in which we do violence: the psychological and institutional as well as physical. In this respect they differ from those who practice nonviolence more selectively. In my introductory classes on nonviolence, we spend the first few classes discussing the nature of violence. Students quickly begin to see that the locus of violence is not in the physical consequences of someone's destructive acts but rather in the mindset that initiates those acts. I ask my students to take note of the violence in the society around them, and when they return to class two or three days later, even though none or few of them have witnessed any physical violence, many of them report how surprised they are by the extent of violence in our culture. It is this sensitivity to the various manifestations of violence—the verbal as well as the physical, the psychological as well as the institutional—that opens the door of awareness about the nature of violence and leads one to a more comprehensive view of how to address violence through a more comprehensive nonviolence.

The physical assaults that most people commonly understand as the paradigm of violence are but a symptom of the doing of violence. They are the most visible symptom, and hence they command the bulk of our attention. But in commanding the bulk of our attention, they distract us from the true locus of the doing of violence. And so the solution to the problem of violence, in part, lies in the ability of a population to identify the doing of violence in all of its manifestations. A sensitization, an awareness, of the nature of doing violence is crucial to generating this solution.

Once one begins to see the many dimensions and faces of violence, one begins to recognize the extent to which we all do violence. And once one realizes the extent to which we all engage in doing violence, to a greater or a lesser extent, one begins to realize that nobody is all good or all bad, that we are all good or bad in varying degrees. Deng Xiaoping, the Chinese leader during the last part of the twentieth century, spoke of Mao Zedong, who to many Chinese has a godlike status and yet is bitterly resented by others, especially those who suffered during the Cultural Revolution of the late 1960s and 1970s. Deng acknowledged Mao's errors—a dangerous thing to do because of the degree to which Mao is revered in China—but Deng pronounced that Mao did more good than harm. He characterized Mao's accomplishments as three-tenths bad and seven-tenths good, and he captured this in a saying: "San qi kai (三 七 开)." It means, literally, a three-seven assessment out of ten. We would say that on a scale of ten he was 30 percent wrong, 70 percent right; 30 percent bad, 70 percent good. Deng Xiaoping meant that Mao was human, neither a god nor a devil. Comprehensive nonviolentists have an easier time accepting this notion than many others, who embrace approaches that tend either to condemn or to praise an entire personality.

Because comprehensive nonviolence identifies the locus of doing violence in the mind of the perpetrator, and because it recognizes us all as capable of doing both good and bad, it also sees little difference between aggressive violence and the violence that people justify in trying violently to put a halt to aggression. Violent defenders introduce violence into the world as much as do violent aggressors even if their actions may be more readily justifiable. But if one's goal is to reduce violence in the world, then one eschews violence, especially since one can never be sure of the consequences of one's violence. And such rejection of violence carries over into the domain of punishment.

We begin by not seeking to punish those whom we believe have done us wrong. People and cultures around the world pay lip service to this alternative approach, but it not really accepted very widely, nor does it run very deep in many places. Unfortunately, the myth that wrongdoers should be punished is so widespread and deeply embedded in so many cultures that most people find absurd the suggestion that wrongdoers *not* be punished. But overcoming the tendency to want to punish is at the heart of comprehensive nonviolence.

REDEMPTION WITHOUT PUNISHMENT

The Navajos have an approach to justice that is restorative and redemptive in nature. It does not call for self-suffering, but it does call for an ability to forgive. It is procedural, attempting to reconcile the wrongdoer both to the truth about his or her wrongdoing and also to the victims of his wrongdoing.

> The parties make their commitment to the process in the opening prayer, and if successful, it concludes with new relationships of respect in which the excuses are exposed as being false and there is a new commitment to an ongoing relationship. The process does not involve coercion or punishment. Navajo thought rejects force and ordering others around. Navajo thought is highly individualistic, with great respect for individual integrity and freedom, yet the process guides people to realize that freedom is exercised in the context of the group and relationships with others. The Navajo maxim is as follows: "He acts as if he had no relatives." At the end of the process, the value of relatives and relationships leads both victim and offender to leave off seeing the world with the head and to instead see it with the heart.[2]

Jesus, Gandhi, Martin Luther King Jr., Leo Tolstoy, and other such comprehensive nonviolentists championed a somewhat different alternative to punishment. They each claimed that suffering can bring redemption, that it can bring fulfillment and reconciliation. But when they spoke of suffering, they were not referring to the suffering of wrongdoers. They were not suggesting that wrongdoers be punished. Nor were they suggesting that wrongdoers be reformed through punishment. They meant something quite different, something almost impossible for most people to take seriously: they meant that wrongdoers are best redeemed by *others'* taking suffering upon themselves for the sake of the wrongdoer; that the way to achieve a better world is for one to be willing to suffer for another, to take responsibility for another, to redeem another through one's own sacrifice.

Jesus, Gandhi, Tolstoy, and King each thought that punishment is *not* an appropriate response to wrongdoers and that taking suffering upon oneself *is* an appropriate response. Gandhi, for example, speaks of fasting as redemptive. Jesus spoke of "turning the other cheek" and, at least according to Christianity, accepted crucifixion as a redemptive act. King often spoke of redemptive self-suffering. Why did these people hold such radically different views from the rest of the world? How can self-suffering be redemptive?

To the extent that a wrongdoer restores what he or she has taken from a victim, some sense of balance, some sense of order is restored. Some degree of redemption is possible. But punishment, strictly speaking, is not what accomplishes this regaining of balance; contrition and restitution do. Shaming wrongdoers, locking them up, executing them, or any other punishment does not, in and of itself, assure a community that order has been restored or that a perpetrator has been redeemed. Sometimes, of course, it may indeed be necessary to restrain a violator to keep order; *then* the restraint *is* somewhat restorative, and then, strictly speaking, it is not punishment, but likely it is not redemptive, either. Contrition, restitution, restoration, and redemption can and do arise without punishment.

Parents are perhaps the best example of people who, ideally, sacrifice for others. Parents sacrifice in all sorts of ways for their children. They forgo spending money on themselves. They forgo taking time to do what they want to do so that they can fulfill their children's wishes. Some parents are faced with the awful choice of sacrificing their very lives for their children's lives, and yet they do it. And with ideal parents, these actions are not done with any self-interest. They are done solely out of love for their children, out of concern for their well-being, out of a concern for doing right by them. If the child feels the love, if the sacrifice—a gift with no guarantee or expectation of success or satisfaction—is not done with a feeling of resentment on the part of the parents, is not done to cover up a parent's shame or embarrassment, then a child who has done wrong is often redeemed.

The balance is delicate. A child, or one's student or charge or friend, can be spoiled as easily as redeemed. One who feels guilt-tripped may develop resentment. Arun Gandhi, a grandson of Mohandas Gandhi, tells a story about an experience he had as a young teen in South Africa. Although he doesn't use the story for this purpose, the story can illustrate the delicate balance between redeeming someone, humiliating them, or creating resentment in them.

Arun Gandhi tells of the time that he and his father, Manilal, drove fifteen miles or so into a nearby city—Durban, I believe—to spend a day running errands there. Arun was entrusted with the car and was responsible for getting it serviced. He was told to meet his father at a particular place and time, and he failed to be there on time. When his father asked why he was late, he lied to his father, who discovered the lie immediately. To punish himself for failing to raise his son properly, his father insisted on walking home rather than riding home with Arun. Arun followed his father home, driving slowly behind him for a number of hours.

From a perspective of nonviolent strategic action, the story is troubling. Ideally, with nonviolent strategic action, a grievance group wants to present an adversary with a choice: "Do as I wish, or make me suffer." However, the suffering that Arun's father took upon himself was not a direct consequence of Arun's choices, decisions, or actions. It was, following a distinction made by Robert L. Holmes, a mediated consequence, the result of a decision made by Arun's father in response to Arun's actions. Holmes defines a mediated consequence of one's actions as a consequence resulting from a decision that another makes in response to one's actions. An unmediated consequence of one's actions is a consequence that results directly from one's actions, regardless of any decisions that another might make.[3] The suffering of Arun's father easily takes on the appearance of a self-inflicted punishment more than that of a straightforward consequence of Arun's actions even if Arun's father suffered from knowing that he had raised a son who would lie to him. However, nonviolent strategy works best when the suffering that one takes upon oneself is not mediated by one's own decisions or actions but rather are unmediated consequences of the actions of those one seeks to convert. Nonviolent activists, at their best, must offer themselves up for suffering, not through a consequence that they mediate, but through unmediated consequences of the actions of those with whom they struggle. But something else is happening here with this example.

It is to Arun Gandhi's credit that he did not receive his father's action as punishment. Knowing his father *was* suffering, not because he chose to walk home but because he was disappointed in the job he had done as a father in raising Arun, Arun resolved never to lie again. Arun instead allowed his father's unmediated response, the disappointment and confusion he felt—and the mediated consequence, the decision to walk home—to work their charm. But other, less noble people would see that self-infliction of punishment as manipulative. Indeed, many parents do manipulate their children through guilt or through fear of their parents' anger or loss of respect for them. In fact, many people see Mohandas Gandhi's various famous fasts as manipulative. But Mahatma Gandhi's fasting is easily misunderstood, as is Manilal Gandhi's decision to walk home, and the fasts that so many others have undertaken in subsequent years, ostensibly following Gandhi's example, bear little if any resemblance in spirit to at least one of the fasts that Gandhi undertook. All that they would seem to have in common is fasting. It is important to understand why Gandhi's fasts were not carried out as manipulative endeavors. It is important to understand why Manilal Gandhi's decision to walk home was not a manipulative endeavor. Understanding why will also enable us to understand an important difference between comprehensive nonviolence and more selective types of nonviolence and nonviolent strategic action.

Gandhi undertook seventeen fasts to the death in his lifetime. Erik Erikson argues that the first of these fasts may well have set the tone for all of Gandhi's later satyagrahic actions.[4] This was the fast that Gandhi undertook at Ahmedabad in 1918. Gandhi had been acting as one of several arbitrators between mill owners and mill workers. He was a friend of the most powerful of the mill owners, and there was thus some suspicion, even hope, that any concessions that might be won from them would be won on the basis of his friendship and not on the basis of any sense of justice on the part of mill owners.[5]

When arbitration essentially failed and the mill owners offered less than what Gandhi considered fair, he urged the workers not to leave to find other work but to stay and strike. He did not wish laborers to be regarded by the owners as migrant workers, and so he extracted from them all a solemn pledge that they would not return to work until their demand for a $0.35 pay raise was met. (The owners had offered $0.20.) After a couple of weeks the strike began to weaken despite Gandhi's daily meetings with five thousand to ten thousand strikers. The strikers saw themselves suffering but saw Gandhi living a relatively comfortable life while he urged them, literally, toward starvation.[6]

At this point Gandhi decided, rather abruptly, to fast, to the death if necessary, not to force mill owners to concede but rather to establish solidarity with the laborers and impress upon them the seriousness of their earlier pledge. Gandhi added:

> [But I am also] aware that [this pledge] carries a taint. It is likely that, because of my vow, the mill-owners may be moved by consideration for me and come to grant the workers' [demand for] thirty-five percent increase. . . . They would do so out of charity and to that extent this pledge is one which cannot but fill me with shame. I weighed the two things, however, against each other: my sense of shame and the mill-hands' pledge. The balance tilted in favour of the latter and I resolved, for the sake of the mill-hands, to take no thought of my shame. In doing

public work, a man must be prepared to put up even with such loss of face. [7]

This quotation reveals, first, that Gandhi neither desired nor aimed at using his fast directly to convert or coerce the opposition to his point of view; he used it to encourage laborers to abide by their pledges, to ensure that generally uneducated people develop and maintain a sense of dignity, especially in the face of their bosses. And he used it to demonstrate to others his own level of commitment to the struggle in which they were engaged. A double effect was at work here: the harm Gandhi did to himself and his reputation on the one hand, and the strength and inspiration he provided the mill workers on the other hand. But it also reveals that the suffering that Gandhi imposed upon himself was aimed at redeeming others as well as at redeeming himself. In this respect it does resemble the actions of his son Manilal toward his grandson Arun. The redemptive act of Arun's father closely matches the conditions that Mohandas Gandhi, Arun's grandfather, had stipulated a few years earlier when aiming to correct wrongdoing through redemptive acts.

Gandhi, who speaks of fasting to redeem wrongdoers in his ashram, for whom he felt responsible, laid down a number of conditions for taking penance upon oneself. In his *History of the Satyagraha Ashram*, Mohandas Gandhi cautions against undertaking fasts, a form of penance, unless these conditions are fulfilled:

1. The wrongdoer should have love for the penitent.
2. The penitent himself must be one of the parties wronged.
3. A penitent for another's wrongdoing must himself be guiltless of similar misconduct.
4. The penitent must otherwise also be a man of purity and appear such to the wrongdoer.
5. The penitent must not have any personal interest to serve.
6. The penitent must not have any anger in him.
7. The wrong act must be patent, accepted as such by all, and spiritually harmful, and the doer must be aware of its nature. [8]

The conditions are interesting in two respects. First, and most relevant to the discussion here, is that this kind of self-suffering *is intended* as a mediated consequence of another's actions. Second, the conditions reflect Gandhi's acute awareness of the difficulties of this kind of self-suffering. As a mediated consequence, the self-suffering will *only* work under these conditions, says Gandhi. Thus, insofar as Gandhi set forth conditions under which one may take penance upon oneself, Gandhi seems to have been very much cognizant, even if only implicitly, of the strategic difference between mediated and unmediated suffering.

Of crucial importance is that if one intends suffering, one can only intend one's own suffering: one might intend to bring about a just system by taunting opponents or damaging their physical property (acts which under certain circumstances some strategic nonviolentists regard as nonviolent), and the effect of that intent might be that one brings about a more just state of affairs. But a reasonably foreseeable consequence of such an action is that the opponents would be harmed. So aside from the potential strategic disvalue of such a consequence, the distinction between mediated and unmediated consequences is relevant here, and it effectively destroys the principle of double effect that is at work in attempting to justify such behavior. The mediated consequence of aiming to damage someone's property or to shame, humiliate, or taunt someone *might* be that a just system obtains; but the unmediated consequence is that one in fact *does* damage, *does* shame, *does* humiliate, or *does* taunt. One only has control of the unmediated consequences of one's actions, not the mediated consequences of one's actions—and *so one cannot justify one's intent on the basis of mediated consequences that are as yet unrealized but desired.* To do so in behaving in an allegedly nonviolent way is no different than U.S. Secretary of Defense Donald Rumsfeld's expressed hope that "shock and awe" bombing would not kill innocent civilians but would bring a quick end to war in Iraq. In the final analysis, it didn't bring a quick end to the war in Iraq, and it did kill innocent civilians. Only the latter could have been reliably predicted. Thus, nonviolent action that is truly nonviolent requires that one's unmediated consequences not be obtained through violence, even psychological or institutional violence, regardless of the mediated consequences that one intends. But selective nonviolence regularly utilizes psychological violence against others and justifies it on the grounds that better mediated consequences will obtain. Gandhi, himself, could be accused of this, but there is a difference: the mediated consequences of Gandhi's actions were exacted upon himself, and only under the seven conditions noted above. Rumsfeld and most of us who justify the violence we perpetrate rarely if ever meet those seven conditions. All too often, the consequences of one's actions are inflicted upon others, and without meeting those seven conditions.

This notion of redemptive suffering occurs elsewhere, most notably in the example of Jesus, who, according to Christians, offered himself as a sacrificial lamb in order to redeem the sins of others. Martin Luther King Jr., too, speaks directly to this idea of redemptive suffering:

> My personal trials have also taught me the value of unmerited suffering. As my sufferings mounted [King is here referring to his arrests, the near-fatal attack upon him early in his career, the bombings of his home] I soon realized that there were two ways that I could respond to my situation: either to react with bitterness or seek to transform the suffering into a creative force. . . . I have attempted to see my personal ordeals as an opportunity to transform myself and heal the people involved in the tragic situation which now obtains. I have lived these last few years with the conviction that unearned suffering is redemptive. [9]

And elsewhere, King says: "The nonviolent approach does not immediately change the heart of the oppressor. It first does something to the hearts and souls of those committed to it. It gives them new self-respect." [10]

Self-suffering is redemptive in several respects. First, it recognizes that both oppressor and oppressed are victims, and it enables both parties to begin to view themselves as capable of doing what is right, responsible for their own fates, and strong enough to effect change. Second, it empowers opponents—as well as the aggrieved party—when opponents may not feel they have power: it offers the opponent a choice and makes the right choice more attractive than it otherwise might be. It does this by holding a mirror up to one's opponents. Gandhi's famous Salt March empowered the Indians to take control of their own lives. Instead of allowing fear to direct their activities, Gandhi and his followers decided what they would do—make salt—and did so, willingly, aware of the possible consequences. It was, in contemporary expression, a proactive move, not a reactive move. For the oppressed group, it was empowering. But on the other hand, it also gave the British a choice and thereby treated them with respect. It said to the British: "Do as we wish, or make us suffer. Respect the ends that we have chosen for ourselves, or look in the mirror and see the extremes to which you will go to keep us from choosing our own ends." The British could stop them only by becoming brutally repressive and seeing themselves as such. Finally, self-suffering can reduce fear in one's opponents because it shows through an unconditional respect for one's opponent, an unwillingness to harm one's opponent. Martin Luther King

Jr. always spoke of this respect in terms of the Greek word *agape*, but it may also be useful to think of it in terms of parental love.

Ultimately, taking suffering upon ourselves is simply another way of acknowledging that we, ourselves, are wrongdoers; and inflicting punishment upon others is simply another way of denying our short-comings as human beings and affirming instead the shortcomings of others. Taking suffering upon ourselves is another way of acknowledging, along with King, that those who perpetrate injustices on others are suffering themselves. It is another way of acknowledging, along with Eugene V. Debs, that "while there is a lower class, I am in it; while there is a criminal element, I am of it; while there is a soul in prison, I am not free." Such sentiments are not sentimentality: they are a conscious recognition that we must embrace a new way of approaching violence, recognizing first, that we can perpetrate violence on others by our nonphysical interactions with them and must avoid doing so when possible; second, that we ourselves can do bad as well as good; third, that the use of violence to prevent violence is counterproductive and rarely justifiable; and fourth, that punishing others really does amount to violence against them.

IF IT'S ABOUT WINNING, IT'S NOT NONVIOLENCE

Imagine then a new scenario, a different cultural perspective than those that dominate today. Imagine people who, when they have caused a great deal of pain to others, come to realize that they have done so, come to realize what they have taken from another. Imagine that they become filled with deep remorse and work genuinely and with repentance, attempting to restore to others whatever they can, or at least working to ensure that they never behave in such a manner again. Imagine injured parties who, instead of insisting on their "rights," instead recognize that the cost of living is sometimes being injured, and that those who injure must be helped to see the pain they cause others, not by punishing them, but, as Plato suggested, by educating them. Such scenarios aren't fiction: they do occur. The question before us is how best to promote them, nonviolently.

A comprehensive nonviolence takes seriously the idea that, in Plato's words, it is better to be injured than to injure. In contemporary language, it is better to take a hit than to make a hit. Why? Because without the willing sacrifice of people committed to a better world, the cycle of violence will simply be perpetuated. Someone, somewhere, must break the cycle, and the more people who are willing to break the cycle, the sooner it will be broken. But it goes beyond the hope that good consequences may result from my choosing not to do violence to another. It goes to the heart of who one is.

"In the end, the most important question one can ask oneself is: What sort of person do I want to be? Do I want to be the sort of person who injures others, who occasionally kills others? Or do I want to be a person who shows faith in the goodness of others, and who is willing to absorb a blow or two rather than deliver one?"[11]

In the *Crito*, Plato's character Socrates states that it is better to be injured than to injure. But as Socrates continues,

> But I would have you consider, Crito, whether you really mean what you are saying. For this opinion has never been held, and never will be held, by any considerable number of persons; and those who are agreed and those who are not agreed upon this point have no common ground, and can only despise one another.[12]

In short, little in history, ancient or modern, suggests that the majority of people will ever adopt the life of nonviolence characterized in this final chapter, but that is not a reason to fail to adopt such a life, or to refrain from trying.

> The exemplary life consists of love and humility; in a fullness of heart that does not exclude even the lowliest; in a formal repudiation of maintaining one's rights, of self-defense, of victory in the sense of personal triumph; in faith in blessedness here on earth, in spite of distress, opposition and death; in reconciliation; in the absence of anger; not wanting to be rewarded; not being obliged to anyone; the completest spiritual-intellectual independence; a very proud life beneath the will to a life of poverty and service.
> —Friedrich Nietzsche, *Will to Power*, 169[13]

NOTES

1. Martin Buber, *I and Thou,* 2nd edition (New York: Charles Scribner's Sons), 1958.

2. James W. Zion, "The Dynamics of Navajo Peacemaking, " *Journal of Contemporary Criminal Justice* 14, no. 1 (February 1998): 58–74, http://iirp.org/library/nacc/nacc_zio.html (accessed on August 2, 2005).

3. Robert L. Holmes, *Basic Moral Philosophy*, 4th edition (Belmont, Calif.: Thomson Wadsworth, 2007), 130 –32.

4. *Satyagraha* is the term that Gandhi used to describe his pursuit of truth through nonviolence. Literally the term means "truth-force" or "holding onto truth."

5. Eric H. Erikson, *Gandhi's Truth: On the Origins of Militant Nonviolence* (New York : W.W. Norton , 1969), 322 –63.

6. Erikson, *Gandhi's Truth*, 338–55.

7. Erikson, *Gandhi's Truth*, 357.

8. Mahatma Gandhi, *A History of the Satyagraha Ashram*, in *The Collected Works of Mahatma Gandhi*, vol. 56: 16 June 1932–4 September 1932, 150–52, http://www.gandhiserve.org/cwmg/cwmg.html (accessed on December 30, 2012).

9. Martin Luther King Jr., *A Testament of Hope, The Essential Writings and Speeches of Martin Luther King, Jr.*, edited by James Washington (New York: Harper Collins, 1991), 41.

10. King, *A Testament of Hope*, 39.

11. Barry L. Gan, "A Philosophy of Peace," in *Peace Movements Worldwide: History, Psychology, Practices*, edited by Michael Nagler and Marc Pilisuk (Santa Barbara, Calif.: Praeger Publishers, 2010), 18–30.

12. Plato, *Crito*, translated by Benjamin Jowett, 49c–d.

13. Friedrich Nietzsche, Will to Power, §169, from http://archive.org/stream/TheWillToPower-Nietzsche/will_to_power-nietzsche#page/n47/mode/2up (accessed on May 16, 2013).

Bibliography

Abernathy, Ralph David. *And the Walls Came Tumbling Down*. New York: Harper & Row, 1989.

Ackerman, Peter, and Jack DuVall. *A Force More Powerful*. New York: St. Martin's Press, 2000.

Amnesty International. "The Death Penalty in 2008." http://www.amnesty.org/en/death-penalty/death-sentences-and-executions-in-2008. Accessed on May 26, 2009.

"Analysis: Otpor's Challenge to Milosevic." *BBC News*. Monday, May 15, 2000. http://news.bbc.co.uk/2/hi/europe/749469.stm. Accessed November 13, 2012.

"The Attack Looms." In *The 9/11 Commission Report*, 215–53. Washington, D.C.: Executive Agency Publications, U.S. Government Printing Office, July 22, 2004.

Benvie, Jan. "Iraq Reflection: The Good, the Bad and the Innocent." August 23, 2005. http://groups.yahoo.com/group/cpt_iraq/message/977. Accessed August 31, 2005.

Berkowitz, L. "The Frustration-Aggression Hypothesis: Examination and Reformulation." *Psychological Bulletin* 106 (1989): 59–73.

"Bringing Down a Dictator." PBS. 2002. http://www.aforcemorepowerful.org/films/bdd/index.php. Accessed on January 7, 2012.

Buber, Martin. *I and Thou*, 2nd ed. New York: Charles Scribner's Sons, 1958.

Bureau of Justice Statistics. U.S. Department of Justice. http://bjs.ojp.usdoj.gov/content/pub/html/cjusew96/cpo.cfm. Accessed on January 7, 2012.

Burger, Jerry M. "Replicating Milgram: Would People Still Obey Today?" *American Psychologist* 64 (January 2009): 1–11.

Burke, Jason. "The Making of the World's Most Wanted Man." *The Observer*. October 28, 2001. http://www.guardian.co.uk/news/2001/oct/28/world.terrorism. Accessed on June 9, 2009.

Bush, George W. Remarks before the Warsaw Conference on Combating Terrorism. November 6, 2001. http://www.washington.polemb.net/sites/embassy_post//Numer4/Numer4_Conference.htm. Accessed on June 14, 2009.

———. State of the Union Address. January 29, 2002. Miller Center, University of Virginia. http://millercenter.org/president/speeches/detail/4540. Accessed on June 8, 2012.

Cady, Duane M. *From Warism to Pacifism: A Moral Continuum*, 2nd ed. Philadelphia: Temple University Press, 2010.

Chenoweth, Erica, and Maria J. Stephan. *Why Civil Resistance Works: The Strategic Logic of Nonviolent Conflict.* New York: Columbia University Press, 2011.

Churchill, Winston. "Blood, Toil, Tears and Sweat" (first speech to the House of Commons). May 13, 1940. Internet Modern History Sourcebook. http://www.fordham.edu/halsall/mod/churchill-blood.html. Accessed on June 15, 2009.

Country Reports of Human Rights Practices for 2007, vol. 1. Washington, D.C.: U.S. Department of State, August 2008.

Deming, Barbara. *Revolution and Equilibrium.* New York: Grossman Publishers, 1971.

"Deterrence: States Without the Death Penalty Have Had Consistently Lower Murder Rates." 2013. Death Penalty Information Center. http://www.deathpenaltyinfo.org/deterrence-states-without-death-penalty-have-had-consistently-lower-murder-rates. Accessed July 2, 2012.

Erikson, Eric H. *Gandhi's Truth: On the Origins of Militant Nonviolence.* New York: W.W. Norton , 1969.

Fanon, Frantz. *The Wretched of the Earth.* New York: Grove Press, 2005.

Farrell, Bryan, and Eric Stoner. "Bringing Down Serbia's Dictator, 10 Years Later: A Conversation with Srdja Popovic." In *Waging Nonviolence.* October 5, 2010. http://wagingnonviolence.orgauthor/bryananderic/. Accessed on November 13, 2012.

Fiala, Andrew. "Pacifism and the Trolley Problem." *The Acorn: Journal of the Gandhi King Society* 15, no. 1 (2013).

Friedman, Thomas. "Make Way for the Radical Center." *The New York Times Sunday Review.* July 23, 2011. http://www.nytimes.com/2011/07/24/opinion/sunday/24friedman.html?_r=1. Accessed January 7, 2012.

"Full text: 'Bin Laden' Tape." *BBC News.* January 4, 2004. http://news.bbc.co.uk/2/hi/middle_east/3368957.stm. Accessed on May 28, 2012.

Gan, Barry L. "Loving One's Enemies." In *Nonviolence in Theory and Practice,* 3rd ed., edited by Robert L. Holmes and Barry L. Gan, 306–13. Long Grove, Ill.: Waveland Press, 2012.

———. "A Philosophy of Peace." In *Peace Movements Worldwide: History, Psychology, Practices,* edited by Michael Nagler and Marc Pilisuk, 18–30. Santa Barbara, Calif.: Praeger Publishers, 2010.

———. Untitled review of Gene Sharp, *Gandhi as a Political Strategist. The Acorn: Journal of the Gandhi-King Society* 5, no. 2 (1991): 27–29.

Gandhi, Mahatma. *The Collected Works of Mahatma Gandhi.* http://www.gandhiserve.org/cwmg/cwmg.html. Accessed January 7, 2012.

———. *A History of the Satyagraha Ashram.* In *The Collected Works of Mahatma Gandhi,* vol. 56: 16 June 1932–4 September 1932, 150–52. http://www.gandhiserve.org/cwmg/cwmg.html. Accessed on December 30, 2012.

Garver, Newton. "What Violence Is." *The Nation* 209 (June 24, 1968): 817–22.

Global Burden of Armed Violence 2008. Geneva Declaration on Armed Violence and Development. http://www.genevadeclaration.org/fileadmin/docs/Global-Burden-of-Armed-Violence-full-report.pdf. Accessed May 26, 2009.

Govier, Trudy. E-mail correspondence . Oct. 30, 2002.

Greenbert, David F., and Biko Agozino. "Executions, Imprisonment and Crime in Trinidad and Tobago." *British Journal of Criminology* 52, no. 1 (2012): 113 –40.

Gregg, Richard B. *The Power of Nonviolence,* 2nd rev. ed. New York: Schoken, 1966.

Grossman, Zoltan. "From Wounded Knee to Iraq: A Century of American Military Intervention." http://academic.evergreen.edu/g/grossmaz/interventions.html. Accessed on May 26, 2009.

Gurr, Ted Robert. "Historical Trends in Historical Trends in Violent Crime: A Critical Review of the Evidence." *Crime and Justice* 3 (1981): 295–353.

Hill, Michael. "Experts Question Wisdom of Sex Offender Restrictions." *The Detroit News*. Associated Press report. June 21, 2005. http://www.detnews.com/2005/politics/0506/21/A04-222081.htm. Accessed June 22, 2005.

History News Network. The Center for History and New Media at George Mason University. June 9, 2003. http://hnn.us/articles/printfriendly/1489.html. Accessed June 2, 2005. As cited in Gan, Barry L. "Pressed Into War." *Peace Review* 17 (Winter 2005): 344–45.

Hitler, Adolf. *Mein Kampf*, vol. 1: A Reckoning, chapter 11: "Nation and Race." http://www.hitler.org/writings/Mein_Kampf/mkv1ch11.html. Accessed on January 7, 2012.

———. *Mein Kampf*, vol. 2: The National Socialist Movement, chapter 14: "Eastern Orientation or Eastern Policy." http://www.hitler.org/writings/Mein_Kampf/mkv2ch14.html. Accessed on January 7, 2012.

———. Speech in the Reichstag on May 4, 1941. http://www.hitler.org/speeches/05-04-41.html. Accessed on June 15, 2009.

Holmes, Robert L. *Basic Moral Philosophy*, 4th ed. Belmont, Calif.: Thomson Wadsworth, 2007.

———. *On War and Morality*. Princeton, N.J.: Princeton University Press, 1989.

———. "Understanding Evil from the Perspective of Nonviolence." *The Acorn: Journal of the Gandhi King Society* 14, no. 1 (Winter–Spring 2010): 5–13.

Hood, Roger. *The Death Penalty: A World-wide Perspective*, rev. ed. Oxford: Clarendon Press, 1996.

Johnson, Paul. *A History of the Jews*. New York: Harper Perennial, 1987.

Kakar, Palwasha. "Tribal Law of Pashtunwali and Women's Legislative Authority." http://www.law.harvard.edu/programs/ilsp/research/kakar.pdf. Accessed June 28, 2012.

"Key Facts at a Glance: Violent Crime Trends, National Crime Victimization Survey Violent Crime Trends, 1973–2008." Bureau of Justice Statistics. http://bjs.ojp.usdoj.gov/content/glance/tables/viortrdtab.cfm. Accessed May 20, 2012.

The King Center. "Six Steps of Nonviolent Social Change." http://www.thekingcenter.org/king-philosophy#sub3. Accessed October 10, 2012.

King, Martin Luther, Jr. "Letter from Birmingham Jail." In *Nonviolence in Theory and Practice*, 3rd ed., edited by Robert L. Holmes and Barry L. Gan, 104–16. Long Grove, Ill.: Waveland Press, 2012.

———. *A Testament of Hope, The Essential Writings and Speeches of Martin Luther King, Jr.* Edited by James Washington. New York: Harper Collins, 1991.

Kirkpatrick, David D., and David E. Sanger. "A Tunisian-Egyptian Link That Shook Arab History." *The New York Times*. February 13, 2011. http://www.nytimes.com/2011/02/14/world/middleeast/14egypt-tunisia-protests.html?pagewanted=all&_r=0. Accessed on November 13, 2012.

Lawson, James. "Nashville." *A Force More Powerful*. PBS. September 2000. http://www.aforcemorepowerful.org/films/afmp/index.php. Accessed on January 7, 2012.

Liptak, Adam. "U.S. Prison Population Dwarfs That of Other Nations." *The New York Times*. April 23, 2008. http://www.nytimes.com/2008/04/23/world/americas/23iht23prison.12253738.html?pagewanted=all. Accessed May 15, 2012.

Milgram, Stanley. "Behavioral Study of Obedience." *Journal of Abnormal and Social Psychology* 67 (1963): 371–78.

"Milosevic: No Signs of Bowing Out." *BBC News*. July 6, 2000. http://news.bbc.co.uk/2/hi/europe/822194.stm. Accessed on November 11, 2012.

Mortimer, Majlinda, and Anca Toader. "Blood Feuds Blight Albanian Lives." BBC News. September 23, 2005. http://news.bbc.co.uk/2/hi/europe/4273020.stm. Accessed June 28, 2012.

Nagler, Michael N. *Is There No Other Way?: The Search for a Nonviolent Future.* Berkeley, Calif.: Berkeley Hills Books, 2001.

Nietzsche, Friedrich. *Will to Power*, §169, from http://archive.org/stream/ TheWillToPower-Nietzsche/will_to_power-nietzsche#page/n47/mode/2up.   Accessed on May 16, 2013.

Ottley, Ted. "Timothy McVeigh & Terry Nichols: Oklahoma Bombing." Crime Library. http://www.trutv.com/library/crime/serial_killers/notorious/mcveigh/updates.html. Accessed on January 7, 2012.

Petrovic, Ivica. "Serbian Non-violence Group Shares Know-how with Egyptian Activists." *Deutsche Welle.* March 28, 2012. http://www.dw.de/dw/article/ 0,,14846311,00.html. Accessed Nov. 10, 2012.

Plato. *Crito.*

Prejean, Sister Helen. *Dead Man Walking.* New York: Vintage Books, 1994.

Rosenberg, Tina. "Revolution U." *Foreign Policy.* February 16, 2011. http://www. foreignpolicy.com/articles/2011/02/16/revolution_u?page=0,0. Accessed on December 3, 2012.

Sacher, Tomas. "The Exporters of Revolution." *Next in Line.* October 10, 2012. http:// nextinline.eu/the-exporters-of-revolution/. Accessed on December 3, 2012.

Sartre, Jean-Paul. "Existentialism Is a Humanism." In *Reason and Responsibility*, 8th ed., edited by Joel Feinberg, 421–28. Belmont, Calif.: Wadsworth, 1993.

Schock, Kurt. *Unarmed Insurrections: People Power Movements in Nondemocracies.* Minneapolis: University of Minnesota Press, 2005.

Schweitzer, Albert. "Albert Schweitzer Speaks Out." A Year Book Special Report from the 1964 World Book Year Book (Chicago: Field Enterprises Educational Corporation, 1964). As cited in *Nonviolence in Theory and Practice*, edited by Robert L. Holmes and Barry L. Gan, 315. Long Grove, Ill.: Waveland Press, 2012.

Sharp, Gene. *Gandhi as a Political Strategist.* Boston: Porter Sargent Publishers, 1979.
———. *The Politics of Nonviolent Action.* Boston: Porter Sargent Publishers, 1973.
———. *Waging Nonviolent Struggle: 20th Century Practice and 21st Century Potential.* Boston: Extending Horizons Books, 2005.

Sivard, Ruth Leger. *World Military and Social Expenditures 1991.* Washington, D.C. : World Priorities, 1991.

Stolberg, Sheryl Gay. "Shy U.S. Intellectual Created Playbook Used in a Revolution." *The New York Times.* February 16, 2011. http://www.nytimes.com/2011/02/17/ world/middleeast/17sharp.html?pagewanted=all. Accessed January 7, 2012.

Thompson, Ernie. "Effects of an Execution on Homicides in California." *Homicide Studies* 3 (1999): 129 –50.

"TIV of Arms Exports from the Top 50 Largest Exporters, 2011–2011." SIPRI Arms Transfers Database, Stockholm International Peace Research Institute. http://www. sipri.org/research/armaments/transfers/databases/armstransfers. Accessed on January 6, 2012.

"Top BJP Man Seeks Gujarat Probe." *BBC News.* May 13, 2005. http://news.bbc.co.uk/ 2/hi/south_asia/4543177.stm. Accessed on June 8, 2012.

Tuchman, Barbara W. *A Distant Mirror.* New York: Alfred A. Knopf, 1978.

"Two Wolves." First People—The Legends. http://www.firstpeople.us/FP-Html-Legends/TwoWolves-Cherokee.html. Accessed on May 28, 2012.

U.S. Department of Education, Institute of Education Sciences. "Revenue and Expenditures for Public Elementary and Secondary Education, School Year 2002–03." http:// nces.ed.gov/ccd/pubs/npefs03/findings.asp. Accessed on June 15, 2009.

"U.S. Spends More per Soldier than Ever Before." MSNBC. February 16, 2005. http:// www.msnbc.msn.com/id/6978975/. Accessed on May 28, 2012.

Wagner, Carl. Guest lectures delivered at St. Bonaventure University in the late 1980s.

Weber, Thomas. "Nonviolence Is Who? Gene Sharp and Gandhi." *Peace & Change* 28, no. 2 (April 2003): 250–70.

Weiner, Neil, et al., eds. *Violence: Patterns, Causes, and Public Policy.* San Diego, Calif.: Harcourt, Brace, Jovanovich, 1990.

Welch, Bud. "Timothy McVeigh Killed My Daughter." Bruderhof Forgiveness Guide. http://www.forgivenessguide.org/articles/Bud-Welch.htm. Accessed June 21, 2005.

White, Matthew. "Source List and Detailed Death Tolls for the Twentieth Century Hemoclysm." http://necrometrics.com/20c5m.htm. Accessed October 10, 2012.

Zimring, Franklin E. "The Scale of Imprisonment in the United States: Twentieth Century Patterns and Twenty-First Century Prospects." *The Journal of Criminal Law and Criminology* 100, no. 3 (2010): 1227–31.

Zion, James W. "The Dynamics of Navajo Peacemaking." *Journal of Contemporary Criminal Justice* 14, no. 1 (February 1998): 58–74. http://iirp.org/library/nacc/nacc_zio.html. Accessed on August 2, 2005.

Index

About the Author

Barry L. Gan is professor of philosophy and director of the Center for Nonviolence at St. Bonaventure University. He is editor of the journal *The Acorn: Journal of the Gandhi-King Society* and has co-edited the anthology, *Nonviolence in Theory and Practice* with Robert L. Holmes.